FAILING

MY WAY TO

SUCCESS

FAILING
MY WAY TO
SUCCESS

Lessons from Forty-Two Years
of Winning (*and Losing*) in Business

PHILLIP CANTRELL

Cheval Press

FAILING MY WAY TO SUCCESS
Lessons from Forty-Two Years of Winning (and Losing) in Business
First Edition

ISBN 978-1-967509-03-4 *Hardcover*
      978-1-967509-02-7 *Paperback*
      978-1-967509-01-0 *eBook*
      978-1-967509-04-1 *Audiobook*

LCCN 2025907744

To my wife Amanda. Not only are you the most loving wife and mother, but your unwavering support and wise counsel over the past twenty-five years have also been key enablers of all my success. Marrying you was indeed a major pivot point of my life. I am convinced that I could never have achieved what I have without you by my side, and in many cases, pushing me from behind. I am blessed to enjoy such a deep partnership. You are my true love and my best friend.

Of equal importance is my gratitude for my savior Jesus Christ, who endowed me with a reasonable amount of talent, wisdom, and discernment—the foundations upon which I have constantly sought to build. Because of these undeserved gifts, I feel an obligation to pay forward what I have learned, and share as much as I can with as many people as possible.

CONTENTS

FOREWORD

In the fall of 2019, after a decade of preparing a platform for consolidating a highly fragmented residential real estate market, my team and I set out to identify well-run companies we could bring onto the platform. Our goal was simple: to realize a return on the investments we had made.

Our process involved identifying the largest and most respected operators in target markets—companies with proven track records of exemplary growth, cultures that put people first, and deep commitments to a higher purpose—and exploring whether they might be good fits. It wasn't easy; for every 100 companies we initially identified as possible prospects, only two or three proved to be ones we wanted to explore moving forward with.

I was introduced to Phillip Cantrell as part of this search by a mutual friend who knew what we were looking for in our prospective "targets." (I put that in quotations because it is impersonal and overly aggressive and does not reflect how I view possible mergers or acquisitions; however, it is the term-of-trade, so I elected to use it here.) This business advisor knew both of us well and thought we viewed our responsibilities to the people who work in our organizations—not to mention to the communities where we operate—similarly. In my opinion, this kind of alignment is essential to a successful transaction and crucial for ensuring the combined businesses perform well post-close, so I was intrigued.

Within minutes of the start of my first conversation with Phillip, it was apparent that he was exceptional. He was and is a humble servant leader. He spoke of the business and his "why" and "how" with such precision and matter-of-fact certainty that I immediately realized that not only did I want to negotiate a transaction that would combine the companies, but that Phillip could significantly impact the broader business. Said plainly, we needed him.

The journey to the closing table was a protracted one due to COVID. We had to delay the planned closing by an initially undetermined amount of time. The adage "time kills deals" is often true, but in this case, the extra time allowed us to take an even deeper look into Phillip's character. His reaction to our notifying him that we needed to pump the brakes on the closing until the world figured out what impact COVID would have was telling. He was even-keeled and understanding. He didn't renegotiate or ask for compensation for the delay. He showed empathy and worked with us to stay positioned to close as the dust settled. All in all, it was an amazing response, and the first of many to come.

Phillip agreed to stay onboard full-time for two years post-transaction to assist with the handoff, then transition to a consultant role. Fast-forward to an offsite leadership meeting in St. Petersburg, Florida a year and a half later, though, and the topic of readying ourselves for Phillip's staged retirement was tabled. In his direct and to-the-point style, Phillip told us there was too much left to do, and he was enjoying his role too much to retire. He graciously agreed to serve the tens of thousands of agents and brokers that call United home by taking on the role of Executive Vice President of Strategy for the entire enterprise while simultaneously (and adeptly) transitioning local operations to a very capable management team.

These stories are important as you begin to read Phillip's first book (I would be shocked if it were his last). As he generously shines a light on his successes, failures, and the lessons he's learned along the way, you'll see for yourself how exceptional he is. He speaks and acts in plain language and actions. I am never confused where Phillip stands with his well-informed and experience-based positions on things. You will discover the same as you turn the pages of *Failing My Way to Success*.

Enjoy the read!

—Dan Duffy
Founder and Chief Executive Officer,
United Real Estate Group

INTRODUCTION

I am an accidental serial entrepreneur. Over the course of a long career, I've founded or controlled ten different companies and engaged in multiple joint ventures. Yet I did not intend any of that when I began. Most of these ventures were simply opportunities that I recognized and chose to pursue along the way. If I were to frame my journey in sports terms with a win-loss-tie record, it would be 4-4-2: four wins, four losses, and two ties. I've taken my fair share of hits, including a few direct shots to the face, only to get back up and swing for the fences again. It's been a process of constant learning—competing fiercely where I had an edge and walking away when I didn't—essentially failing my way to success.

In late 2020, Benchmark Realty, the company my wife Amanda and I founded nineteen years ago, was acquired by the seventh largest real estate brokerage organization in the US. Though technically an employee now, I remain in a leadership position at Benchmark.

I recently returned from the annual leadership meeting in Dallas where the parent company brings together both franchise owners and leaders of their corporately-owned operations like Benchmark. The goal: to cross-pollinate, share ideas, and help each other grow. I quickly realized I was an anomaly in that room. Benchmark has 1,750 or so agents and will sell around $5 billion worth of real estate this year. In addition to numerous other honors, we have been independently ranked on the *Inc. 5000* list for multiple years. Meanwhile, the average attendee at this meeting had about fifty agents. A broad disparity in size, for sure.

You might think companies operating on such different levels wouldn't have much in common. However, what struck me was that there are indeed common threads—the same principles that work for us could absolutely work for them. Those smaller teams, those fifty-agent team leaders and company owners, can use the very same strategies and tactics that we use in order to push through challenges. There's nothing stopping them from growing and becoming more profitable, *if* they're willing to cultivate the right mindset and put forth the effort.

The same goes for you. If you're content staying small, that's fine. But if you want to grow your business—if you want to make a real impact in your community—you *can* do it. It might just take someone giving you a swift kick in the butt, which is what I hope to do for you in this book.

The people I admire the most—the entrepreneurs I have met along the way who have done the best—all have something in common: their mindset. They *believe* in their ability to execute, and if you want the same kind of success they have, you have to do the same. I can give you all the advice in the world on how to scale your business, but if you don't *believe* you can do it, all that advice is just white noise.

In the Dallas meeting I just told you about, a lot of people in that room struggled to envision a path that would take them from where they are now to where I am today. But here's the thing—I didn't start here. I didn't start with 1,750 agents and a multi-billion-dollar operation. I started by humbling myself at the lowest rung of the ladder. I went to a guy and said, "I'll work for you for free. Just teach me everything you know about this business." I was willing to admit what I didn't know and willing to completely open my mind to learn from someone who did. That level of humility is foundational for success. However, as I know firsthand, it's not always easy, especially when you've spent much of your life feeling like you have something to prove.

Growing up, my brother was the intellectual one. I was the athlete. There was always that comparison, and it would have been easy for me to let pride take over, refuse to listen, and never learn a single thing. But I knew where I could compete. I knew I wasn't going to win in academics, but I always knew I could win in my own vertical, in my chosen path, in my own lane.

I've discovered the hard way to never try to compete with others in their areas of strength. I focus on competing with myself in my own vertical. I'm driven by a simple mantra: "The only person I'm competing with is the man I shave with every morning." Once I chose to place my focus there, the rest of the noise faded away.

This philosophy has served me well. It's carried me through challenges both personal and professional, and it continues to be my north star today. It's the philosophy I've tried to impart to the people I've mentored over the years, and it's one that you'll see crop up again and again in these pages.

This book leans heavily on my own stories and experiences, as well as the family history that ultimately shaped the man I became, but it isn't intended to be a memoir. Instead, I'm going to pull key strategies out of my life to show you how to make an impact in your business and *your* life. That said, this isn't a book that's solely about business strategies or best practices. At its heart, it's about developing the mindset to win in your own lane, to push yourself beyond what you think is possible, and to ignore the comparisons that are holding you back.

Learning from the wisdom of those who have come before us seems to be a lost art in society today. Gen Z finds no use for what Millennials learned. Millennials have no use for the collective knowledge of Gen X or Boomers, and so on. That's a mistake. The importance of collective wisdom was summed up well by Colin Powell when he said, "There are no secrets to success. It is the result of preparation, hard work, and learning from failure." Hopefully you can learn from my failures...and avoid them. Hopefully, you can thrive on your own journey to greater success.

Helping my fellow entrepreneurs succeed—helping *you* succeed—is one of my driving forces now. It's why I've worked so hard on this book. So, let's get started.

RESILIENCE AND GRIT

UTHOR B.J. NEBLETT ONCE OBSERVED THAT WE are the sum total of our experiences. Reflecting on my own life, I recognize that a different path would have led to a very different outcome—perhaps one less successful. But beyond our individual experiences, I believe we are also deeply shaped by our family history...what some may call our "roots." Understanding those roots is key to understanding our future.

My roots run deep with resilience. I come from a long line of people who faced significant challenges and hardships, yet persevered. According to my father's research, a Cantrell with the rank of Major served in the Revolutionary Army and was awarded 500 acres in the DeKalb County area of Tennessee as compensation for his service. He had nine sons, and from them, our family name spread. Even today, you can still see the Cantrell name on mailboxes and businesses throughout that region.

In the early 19th century, some members of the Cantrell family moved from DeKalb County to the Nashville area, settling near the Cumberland River on Bull Run Road in the western part of Davidson County (now part of greater Nashville). My great-great-grandfather, Lafayette Cantrell—known to the family as "Fate"—was a modest farmer. Although he passed away long before my time, I have vivid memories from my childhood of visiting the two-room log cabin he built in the early 1800s, and I still have some of the handmade iron spikes from its construction. Lafayette married June, her maiden name lost to history, and they had five children.

Their firstborn, my great-grandfather James Knox Polk Cantrell, remained in the valley, marrying Louisa Simpkins in the late 1860s. They had six children. Tragically, James died young, likely in his late thirties, after contracting pneumonia while building a small church. Of their six children, the one who matters most to me is Dave Lee Cantrell. Born on March 31, 1890, he was my grandfather and the first of four Dave Lee Cantrells in our family line. My father always referred to him as "DLC Sr."

DLC Sr. had two brothers and two sisters, but after their father's early death, none stayed in the Bull Run area for long. Forced to fend for themselves at a young age, they made their way to the nearby big city of Nashville, where some of them found employment in the commercial printing industry. While Nashville is often associated with the music industry, it was once a major hub for printing, largely due to religious publishers like Thomas Nelson, the United Methodist Publishing House, the Baptist Sunday School Board (now Lifeway), and others.

Despite the economic hardships of the Great Depression, DLC Sr. always found work—something that wasn't true for many in those difficult times. Sadly, I never got to meet him, as he passed away in 1940 at the age of fifty. His lifestyle likely contributed to his early death—he smoked two packs of cigarettes a day and drank a lot of whiskey. He lived life fast, but he seems to have been well-liked and known for being fun to be around. Nearly everyone in the family followed him into the printing business, including my father, Dave Lee Cantrell Jr., who began his career in the press room and later moved into a sales assistant and administrative role. After some years, my father was able to work his way into outside sales and, later, a sales management role. Eventually, he became Vice President of Marketing & Sales.

My father had dropped out of school in the tenth grade because he felt suffocated by my grandmother's overprotectiveness following my grandfather's death. Plus, his family needed the money he could earn working—opportunities were limited for single mothers in the 1940s. Eager for the independence that earning his own wages would bring, he went to work at sixteen as an errand boy for an old Nashville original, General Shoe Company—now known as Genesco (the parent company of such brands as Johnson & Murphy). A year or so later, he went to work at the commercial printing company I described above.

Like that of so many people, his path had twists and turns. When World War II broke out, my father was too young to enlist, and by the time he was finally drafted, the war was nearing its end. He completed boot camp and infantry training, but the war concluded before he shipped out overseas. Nevertheless, he stayed in the Army Reserves, and when the Korean War began, he was called back to active duty and assigned to a services company.

At that point, fate took an unexpected turn. While transitioning through Fort Lewis, Washington, preparing to ship out to Korea, my father's unit was billeted next to a Graves Registration unit (which was tasked with recovering soldiers' remains after battles). The night before deployment, two men from that unit went AWOL, and my father was "volunteered" by his commanding officer to take their place. Without a choice, he found himself in Korea, working in Graves Registration for the next eighteen months.

Many of the soldiers in the unit were morticians, trained to handle death. But my father had no such background. He was just a young man who wanted to serve his country. He knew that there were many ways to do that in the military, and that at the end of the day, you do what you're told. And so, that's what he did.

While in Korea, he handled both administrative and field duties, occasionally venturing close to combat zones to retrieve bodies. There were times when his unit operated perilously close to active battles. In fact, I can remember him telling me about several occasions when combat was taking place just over the hill from where his unit was working. As the combat units pressed forward, his unit moved in behind to recover and process the battle casualties to return them to their loved ones back home. Though he only came under fire a few times, it was a dangerous environment and the work was, to put it mildly, highly stressful. Despite this, my father excelled in his role. His work ethic caught the eye of his new commanding officer, Lieutenant Binkley, who planned to recommend him for a battlefield commission—an opportunity to rise through the ranks.

However, there was one major obstacle. One day, Lieutenant Binkley called my father into his tent after reviewing his personnel file. "Cantrell, I've been looking at your records, and I think you're the biggest dumbass I've ever met," Binkley said in so many words. He couldn't believe my father didn't even have a high school education. Despite my father's exceptional performance, he lacked the minimum educational credentials required to receive a commission. But rather than simply reprimanding him, Binkley became a mentor. He encouraged my father to earn his GED when he returned home, and my father took that advice to heart.

As soon as he rotated back to the States, my father earned his GED. He didn't stop there, though: He went on to earn an associate's degree in business by attending night school at the University of Tennessee in Nashville, all while working full-time as the sole provider for a family of four. Some people might have viewed his circumstances as a debilitating handicap, but he viewed it as a challenge to improve himself. That determination is something that defined him and, I believe, runs deep in our family.

In fact, as I reflect on my father's story—and my entire family's history, from the Revolutionary War to the Great Depression, and from World War II to Korea—two defining qualities stand out: **resilience** and **grit**. Through every challenge, they did what needed to be done, regardless of how difficult or unpleasant it might be. This unwavering determination has been passed down through the generations. My family was not immune to hardship, but they *always* found a way to persevere, even in the face of daunting circumstances. And in many ways, those same qualities have shaped who I am today.

A SENSE OF LOYALTY

On my mother's side, the challenges were different, but no less formidable. My maternal great-grandparents were near-destitute farmers in Cheatham County, one of Tennessee's poorest areas. Seeking to escape that life, my grandparents married young—my grandfather was eighteen and my grandmother just sixteen. Together, they had seven children, though tragedy struck early: one child died during childbirth, and another passed away at the age of nine. Despite these hardships, my grandmother focused on raising the five surviving children (one of whom was mentally handicapped) while my grandfather worked for the US Army Corps of Engineers, helping to maintain various river locks and dams in the area.

Life was far from easy. My mother and her siblings grew up in homes without indoor plumbing. My grandmother stayed home, tending to the garden, chickens, and children—likely in that order, knowing her. Eventually, my grandfather transitioned from working on the locks to cutting grass for the Corps of Engineers, requiring the family to move around various parts of Middle Tennessee—Cheatham County, Trousdale County, and others—until he retired at sixty-two. Unfortunately, his retirement was short-lived; he passed away just two years later from a stroke. Both of my grandfathers died relatively young, and as I reflect on their lives, it's a bit sobering to realize I've already lived longer than both of them.

One of the more remarkable legacies my maternal grandfather left behind is tied to his work with the Corps of Engineers. While maintaining the locks, he planted several pecan trees at a recreation area near one of the locks he helped maintain. Many of those trees are still there today. I've visited them: placed my hands on their bark and felt a tangible connection to my family's history. And that's not the only connection I've felt. The house where my grandparents lived sat on a bluff overlooking the river in an elevated spot because the valley flooded frequently before the dam was built. The last time I visited there, the foundations of the government housing for workers like my grandfather were still visible.

Every spring, buttercups bloom where the yards of these homes once stood—a simple yet beautiful reminder of the lives that once flourished there. Interestingly, buttercups often grow where homes once existed, even long after the buildings are gone. If you ever find yourself in a forested area and spot a patch of buttercups in a seemingly odd location, there's a good chance that a house once stood there. Like the trees my grandfather planted, these flowers serve as quiet markers of human history and resilience.

My parents eventually achieved a solid middle-class life, but that outcome was far from easy or guaranteed. The journey from generational poverty to financial stability was anything but straightforward. My family came from nothing—both sets of great-grandparents were poor farmers, living in the extreme poverty of rural Tennessee, with every reason to believe the cycle would continue. My grandparents did slightly better, but not much. Yet my parents made a conscious decision to break free from that path.

My mother, in particular, sought escape early on. At sixteen or seventeen, she left home and entered a brief marriage, more as an exit strategy than a romance. That union lasted only several months, and there were no children. Some years later, after my father returned from Korea, they met and married. Technically, my dad was her second husband, but that first marriage was more a pathway out of her difficult circumstances than any sort of true partnership. I think that decision was a burden for her the rest of her life.

Upon leaving her first husband, my mother moved from Hartsville to Nashville and found work as a telephone operator for Bellsouth, in the days before technology replaced such jobs. She lived in a boarding house (located on 16th Avenue South) run by a widow named Jennie B. Simmons. Ms. Simmons had transformed the upstairs of her home into a sanctuary for young, single women, offering them safety and support. My mother lived there until she married my father, and Ms. Simmons became like a third grandmother to my brother and me. We knew her simply as "Nana." She wasn't just a landlord; she cared for the women who lived there like a mother and remained an extended part of our family until her sad passing in the early 1980s.

That sense of loyalty and familial connection runs deep in our family. Perhaps it's even part of the fabric of Tennessee culture. We may argue amongst ourselves, but the moment someone from outside tries to interfere, we close ranks and would fight the devil himself to defend each other. It's an unspoken rule: I can criticize my brother, but if someone else does, they'll have to answer to me. That tight-knit bond and fierce loyalty have been a defining force in our family's resilience and success over the years.

It's this combination of grit, resilience, and loyalty that has helped my family navigate challenges and build a better life, generation after generation. These traits have not only helped us survive difficult times but have also been instrumental in enabling us to achieve ever-greater success.

TWO

FINDING MY OWN PATH

ROWING UP, I WASN'T EXACTLY THE ACADEMIC standout in my family. That title belonged to my brother, who went on to become Dr. Cantrell, a professional geologist with a PhD from the University of Manchester (yep, the one in England). He is literally off-the-charts brilliant in his chosen field.

I may not have been the academic star, but I was scrappy. While my brother was buried in books, I craved action. Sitting still never came naturally to me. I was the kid climbing trees, playing football, and jumping off roofs. In fact, I was so "active" that even before the age of eleven, I had made five separate trips to the emergency room to have my face stitched up from various falls or collisions with immovable objects. It happened a few times after my eleventh birthday too, although as I matured, I learned to not lead with my head as much. Unlike my brother, who thrived in quiet, focused environments, academic pursuits didn't hold my attention.

By the time I finished elementary school, things were changing in Nashville with the introduction of busing as part of the integration efforts in the south. While well-intentioned, it wasn't logistically practical for our family. My zoned middle school would have required more than a forty-five-minute bus ride each way, and my parents were not willing to subject me to that. Spending ninety minutes a day on a bus just wasn't an option.

So, they decided to send both my brother and me to Montgomery Bell Academy (MBA), an all-boys private school with a strong academic reputation in Nashville. My brother started in ninth grade, and I entered seventh grade in 1971. It turned out to be a pressure cooker, and a very negative experience for me in many ways.

While my brother excelled academically at MBA, I struggled. Even with a tutor, I had a hard time staying engaged with the school's rigorous academic focus. At the end of that year, the school asked my parents to come in for a meeting. The head of the middle school acknowledged I wasn't a troublemaker—after all, I had only been sent to the principal's office twice, which they considered pretty good. But then came the tough conversation. MBA gave my parents an ultimatum: Because my academic performance had fallen short of their standards, I could either repeat the seventh grade at the academy or they'd give me enough credits to move on to the eighth grade *at another school*. In short, they were offering my parents an easy way to move me out.

I wasn't a bad kid; I just didn't like to sit still and focus for long. Today, I'd probably be labeled ADHD or something similar, but back then, my behavior was simply seen as disruptive. The standard admonition to "sit down and be quiet" was never going to work for me. So, my parents decided to move me to another private school, Battleground Academy (BGA) in Franklin, which at the time was known for its strict discipline, bordering on a military academy—something they thought would "cure" me of my restless behavior.

To get in, I had to take an entrance exam. I remember sitting in the foyer before the test, looking around at the class pictures on the walls while waiting to be called into the testing room. That's when it hit me—there were no girls in the pictures! *BGA was an all-boys school too!* The last thing I wanted at that age was another boys-only environment. So I only half-heartedly took the exam, and unsurprisingly, I didn't get in…much to my relief. *(Sorry-not-sorry, Mom and Dad.)*

That's how I ended up at Nashville Christian School. When busing began in Nashville, several local churches responded by starting private schools, and Nashville Christian was one of them. It was co-ed, and for me, that was a major upgrade. Finally, a school where I could feel more at ease—and it ended up being the right fit for me. At the time I enrolled, NCS offered just first through eighth grades, but added one grade each year going forward. Since I joined in my eighth grade year, this meant that my classmates and I were essentially seniors our entire high school education. What an incredible bonus!

Looking back, I realize that my experience of moving from school to school taught me invaluable lessons about adapting to new environments. It also reinforced something I had always known about myself: I thrive on action, movement, and a hands-on approach to life. When I didn't get into Battleground Academy, my parents were understandably disappointed, but I couldn't have cared less. I had been labeled a "strong-willed child" for most of my life, and this was just another moment that highlighted how I didn't fit the mold of others' expectations of me.

Undoubtedly, some of that stubbornness stemmed from growing up in the shadow of my brother. He was the classic rule-follower, the "ideal" kid everyone praised. In elementary school, teachers would occasionally remind me (sometimes with a smile bordering on a sneer), "I had your brother in my class. It's surprising that you aren't more like him." That only added fuel to my fire. My internal response was always, "Forget about my brother. I'm my own person." It didn't help that even my mother echoed this sentiment at times, once saying outright, "Why can't you be more like your brother?" To be clear, I knew that none of this was his fault. It was nothing more than the ignorance of those who refused to accept that we were each our own person.

Instead of falling in line, I doubled down on being rebellious. "Tell me I can't do something and I'll do it twice and take pictures" was my motto. If they thought I was being difficult before, I'd show them just *how* difficult I could be. I was a fighter—physically and mentally. I got into plenty of scrapes, and it's a wonder I still have all my teeth. But that defiant streak became a core part of my identity. You might knock me down, but you'd know you had been in a real dogfight when it was over.

That scrappiness, while a defining trait, also created a lot of tension between my mother and me. I loved her deeply, and undoubtedly she loved me, but we were wired so differently. She grew up with a rigid, black-and-white worldview, heavily influenced by her father, and she didn't know how to handle my rule-breaking, restless spirit.

As difficult as our relationship could be at times, I am forever grateful that there was a final moment of reconciliation between my mother and I that changed—and, in many ways, healed—everything. When she was in hospice, nearing the end of her battle with pancreatic cancer, Dad and I sat by her bedside every day. She was often unconscious, heavily sedated on morphine. But two days before she passed, with my dad out of the room for some reason, she suddenly gained some lucidity, looked me in the eye, and said, *"Phillip, I'm sorry for everything I've ever done to you, and I hope you'll forgive me."*

That moment hit me like a ton of bricks. It was as if a lifetime of unspoken feelings had surfaced in those few words. Even now, thinking about it, I get emotional. In that instant, everything between us shifted, and the weight of years of tension melted away. It was the closure I didn't realize I needed until that very moment.

My heartfelt response to the final words she ever said to me: *"I already have, Mom."*

TOUGHNESS VERSUS SOFTNESS

To be fair to my mother, life hadn't been easy for her. That was true for her parents as well, especially her father, and generational traits tend to surface in all lineages. He was raised by a stepmother who kicked him out of the house when he was still very young. From that point on, he had to fend for himself, living on the streets and relying on the kindness of strangers. That experience hardened him in many ways.

Funny enough, despite his rough exterior, he had a real soft spot for me. Maybe it was because we shared the same middle name—he was Robin Clay, I am Phillip Clay—but I was clearly his favorite grandchild. No matter what, I could do no wrong in his eyes. Yet, even with that bond, there was no denying the sharp edge he carried with him. Life had made him tough, and that toughness left little room for warmth.

On the other hand, my grandmother—his wife—was the complete opposite. Her name was Dovie, but I often called her "Dovie Lovie," a nickname she truly lived up to in so many ways. Others may not have seen her this way, but in my eyes she was the kindest, gentlest person I've ever known, and her love was unconditional. Even today, I smile when I think of her, and I get a warm feeling at the thought of seeing her again someday when the good Lord calls me home. She showed me what real love looks like, even when life wasn't particularly kind to either of us.

Fortunately, I didn't inherit my grandfather's hardness, at least not in the same way. While I have an edge—I don't let people walk all over me—I never built the kind of impenetrable walls that he did. A big part of that, I think, comes from my Christian faith and my belief that everyone, at their core, wants to be loved.

Looking back, a lot of my rebellious behavior when I was younger—whether it was causing trouble or pushing boundaries—was probably my way of seeking attention, trying to feel like I mattered. Over time, I've come to understand this about myself, though in the moment, I didn't always understand why I acted or reacted the way I did.

There's a time and a place for being tough, but that doesn't mean you have to be hard-hearted. One of the biggest lessons I've learned over the years is that you can stand your ground without being a jerk. You can call out someone's bad behavior or even tell them they're acting foolishly, as long as you deliver that message in the right way. That said, I am a strong believer in direct speech so that there are no misunderstandings.

The way you communicate makes all the difference. You want to get your point across in a way that allows people to really hear you, rather than putting up defenses. That's always been my goal—to speak the truth in a way that ensures the message is received. It's not about being soft; it's about being smart in how you lead and how you communicate.

In many ways, I walk the line between my grandfather's toughness and my grandmother's softness. Together, they taught

me that you can be strong without being hardened, and that's
the approach I've tried to carry with me throughout my life.

SOMETHING TO PROVE

Ultimately, my upbringing made me feel like I had something to
prove, and I've come to realize that people with that mindset are
usually the ones who often achieve the highest levels of success.
The need to prove themselves drives them, pushes them to keep
moving forward, and fuels their ambition.

I'll be the first to admit I wasn't the smartest person in the
room, and I definitely wasted plenty of opportunities, especially
in college. But I'm living proof that you don't need a perfect GPA
to become successful. In fact, I became a multimillionaire with
just a 2.6 GPA—and honestly, I was lucky to earn that. Truth be
told, if I hadn't buckled down in my final year of college, I might
not have even achieved that modest average.

My first year at the University of Tennessee in Knoxville was
rough. I finished my first quarter with a 1.6 GPA and barely
improved it to 1.9 by the second quarter. I was on academic proba-
tion and teetering on the edge of once again being asked to leave
an educational institution. Thankfully, with some manipulation
of my course load, I managed to scrape together a 2.0 by the end
of freshman year, which is the only reason I was allowed to stay.

Looking back, I can own up to the fact that my struggles in college were largely self-inflicted. I partied too much and didn't take my responsibilities seriously. Once you dig yourself into an academic hole like that, it's tough to climb out. I spent a lot of time playing intramural sports and drilling with my Army ROTC unit, and if beer drinking had been a competitive event, I'd have made All-Conference. I let so many valuable opportunities slip away during those years.

One of my biggest regrets from college was dropping out of ROTC. During my first year and a half, I was all in. I wanted to become a career military officer. For the first two years of ROTC there is no legal commitment, since that comes at the end of year two. But when it came time to sign the papers and make that commitment, I balked. Yet, even after starting my printing company, the desire to serve never left me. Eventually, I joined the Naval Reserve, serving in a naval aviation supply unit. Once the Navy hitch was complete, I moved over to the Army National Guard and was assigned to a unit that ended up being activated during the first Persian Gulf War. Technically, I'm a Desert Storm veteran with eight years of military experience, but many others did far more than me in service to our country.

I want to be clear that I wasn't drafted—I chose to serve because I felt a strong sense of responsibility and patriotism. My father, grandfather, and great-grandfather were all veterans, and

I held myself to the same standard. Earning my veteran status was important to me, another thing I felt I needed to prove. And I'm glad I did. That drive to live up to a certain ideal has been in me from the start.

When I reflect on my journey—the challenges, the mistakes, and the work ethic I developed—I wouldn't change much about any of it. The relentless determination that led to any success I've found came directly from those experiences. It wasn't easy, and often it was painful and frustrating. But I'm grateful. Those hard times shaped the person I am today. I truly believe that without those struggles, my outcomes would have been far more mediocre.

THREE

TACKLING PROBLEMS HEAD-ON

WHEN IT CAME TO BUILDING A BUSINESS, MY FAMily didn't have an inherited legacy—we forged our own. Case in point: My father didn't start out as the owner of a printing company. His journey toward eventual entrepreneurship began in the press room at Williams Printing Company, one of Nashville's largest printing firms at the time. As I mentioned earlier, he eventually worked his way up to Vice President of Sales & Marketing. However, despite his success, by the time I was in college, he had begun to feel constrained in that role. He had achieved so much, yet he yearned for more.

During my senior year at UT, my father and I had several conversations about my post-graduation plans. I was pursuing a business degree and had a growing interest in entrepreneurship. The more we talked about it, the more it became clear that we shared a common vision: We both wanted to start something of our own.

What began as a humble venture—just my father and me—soon evolved into something much greater. We lacked substantial resources, so we relied on determination and grit to lay the foundation for a business that would ultimately shape our family's future.

Realizing that I had a lot to learn about the particulars of the printing industry, I spent a fair bit of time thinking about how I could get hands-on experience after graduating. Eventually, I had an idea: I approached a long-time family friend, Jimmy Duty, who owned Duty Printing Company. Jimmy and my father had known each other since high school and had collaborated on various business ideas over the years. I proposed a deal.

"Jimmy, I understand the business side—accounting, finance, inventory management, and such—but I need to learn how to run a press," I told him. I offered to work for him without pay in exchange for him teaching me everything he knew about operating a printing company.

For the next three months, I worked for free, absorbing everything Jimmy had to teach me. And then one day, he called me into his office and said, "I can't do this anymore."

Confused (and instantly thinking I had made some terrible mistake), I asked, "What do you mean?"

"You're adding too much value to my business, and I can't continue without compensating you," he explained with a smile. "I have to put you on the payroll."

At the time, I was living at home with no significant expenses, so I replied, "Whatever you want to pay me is fine." So, he started paying me, and I continued working for him for several more months, soaking up as much knowledge as I could.

Eventually, my father and I knew it was time to take the next step. We purchased some printing equipment and set it up in the basement of my parents' home. That's how Cantrell Graphics came to life—a venture built on the hard-earned knowledge, persistence, and drive that defined our family's entrepreneurial spirit.

For the first year or so after we launched, my dad continued working at Williams Printing Company. To help us get off the ground, he would send over small, odd jobs, while I leveraged his network to sell printing services to other clients and slowly expanded our base. I handled every aspect of the process—selling the job, pre-press, printing, trimming, binding, and delivering—before heading out to secure the next order. Sometimes, I worked until one or two o'clock in the morning to complete production on a job facing a tight deadline. Then, I'd turn around and do it again the next day. It was a grind, but it was exactly what we had to do to grow the business, and we both thrived on the challenge.

We operated out of that basement for about two years, and during that time, we experienced steady growth. We hired our first employee, needed to hire a second, and soon it became clear that we were outgrowing the space. I began to seriously contemplate what the next phase of my life—and the next phase of the business—looked like. After giving it a lot of thought, I knew what I wanted to do, but I also knew I needed to get my dad's buy-in. So, I sat down with him for one of the most important conversations of my life.

"We need to make a decision," I told him. "Either we both go full-time with this, or we let it go, and I'll move on to something else."

We decided to take the plunge.

We moved the business into a rented commercial space and, over time, expanded Cantrell Graphics to a team of six employees. For the next five years, we worked hard and built the company together. But, as often happens in family businesses, challenges arose. As a young twenty-something, my energy and ambition were increasing, while my dad, who was in his late fifties, was starting to slow down. It led to mounting frustrations for both of us. That's when I learned one of the most important lessons of my life: **family and business don't always mix well.**

To preserve our relationship, we decided to sell the company. Both of us agreed to stay on with the acquiring firm for a while, but it quickly became apparent that this new situation wasn't a good fit for me. The new owners were, quite frankly, poor businesspeople, and after six months, I knew I had to move on. I left to join another local printing company and continue building my career in the industry.

We sold Cantrell Graphics in 1988, closing that chapter of my career, but the lessons I learned during those early years proved invaluable. One of the most significant takeaways was that avoiding conflict and stress leads to mediocrity. In business, you can't shy away from challenges—you have to tackle them head-on.

NOTHING'S GOING TO STOP ME

When I was younger, I struggled with the physical manifestations of stress, which resulted in severe cystic acne that scarred my face, chest, and back. When people asked me about the scars later in life, I usually fibbed and told them I had been in a car wreck and gotten thrown through the windshield. It really was that bad. The cysts were painful—some as large as the tip of my thumb. Playing football in high school and wearing those shoulder pads would often bring tears to my eyes because of the pressure on the cysts. But I had a drive to play, to compete, and to be the best I could be, so I learned to suck it up and push through the immense pain.

By my senior year of high school, I was 5'10 ½", weighed 198 pounds, and had a 30-inch waist. Muscular for sure, but definitely not the size of a typical defensive end. But I earned my spot as the starting defensive end on my private school's team simply because no one could stop me coming around the end of that offensive line. Yes, we were playing other private schools, not NFL teams, but remember that grit and never-say-die attitude I told you about? Well, I had resolved that *nothing*—not pain, not doubters, and certainly not someone bigger than me— was going to hold me back. That mindset was foundational to my successes on the football field, and it would be foundational to my success in business.

One football tackle drill I often think about illustrates this well. In that drill, two players would line up facing each other, one holding the ball, the other set to tackle. At the sound of the whistle, we'd run straight at each other, as hard as we could, from a distance of about fifteen feet. I quickly realized that even the slightest hesitation before contact made the impact hurt far more. Sure, running headfirst at another guy was going to be painful, but if you committed fully—lowered your head and drove all the way through the other player—you could minimize the pain. The same philosophy is true in business: Whatever the challenge, face it head-on. Run as hard at the problem as you possibly can. Don't avoid it. Don't hesitate. Don't make excuses. Because I promise you: the longer you avoid a problem, the bigger it becomes, and eventually, avoiding the problem will hurt far more than putting your head down and driving through it.

This approach extends beyond business challenges to managing personal conflicts. Our natural instinct is to pull back when we encounter discomfort or pain. But I've learned that the best path forward is to push through, to tackle problems directly. Yes, it might hurt in the moment, but once you're on the other side, the pain dissipates.

In business, it's easy to fall back on excuses—whether it's the economy, an election year, or any number of external factors. These excuses sound reasonable at the moment, and the more we repeat them, the more we believe them. But the truth is, recognizing those excuses for what they are and deciding instead to run straight at the problem, no matter how painful it seems, is always the better choice.

This is where tenacity plays a critical role. To succeed in business, you need to develop a certain level of toughness—a mindset that says, "I'm not giving up." It's like ripping off a Band-Aid:

Whether you pull it slowly or quickly, it's going to hurt the same. You might as well rip it off quickly and deal with the brief pain. It's the same with life. You must find the resilience to endure the tough moments, absorb the hits, and keep moving forward.

KILLING THE MAGNIFICENT STAG

In business, much like in football, you'll inevitably face challenges that seem insurmountable. But if you commit to pushing through the discomfort and tackling issues head-on, you'll emerge stronger on the other side. It's about adopting an unwavering mindset that says, "You may defeat me, but you will *never* outwork me. You may get the best of me, but when it's over, there *will* be blood on the ground, and you'll *know* we were in a fight." Without this level of resolve, the demands of business will wear you down.

Yet here's a key point: toughness alone isn't enough. You need to be strategic about when to engage and when to not engage. As Sun Tzu famously taught, you have to pick your battles wisely. Fight when you must, but retreat when it's prudent. If you can avoid useless or unnecessary conflict, do so. But when a decision is unavoidable, face it directly and get it done.

This principle applies across the board, whether you're dealing with an underperforming employee, a problematic client, or a toxic colleague. Do not avoid the tough conversations.

I'm reminded of Winston Churchill during World War II, when British forces were struggling against Rommel's advance in North Africa. Despite General Auchinleck's impressive credentials, medals, and noble pedigree, he wasn't delivering the results the situation required. Churchill made the difficult decision to replace him with General Montgomery, who eventually turned the tide and led the British to victory.

It must have been an agonizing decision: Churchill described replacing Auchinleck as feeling like "killing a magnificent stag." But he knew it had to be done for the greater good. That's the reality of leadership and business. Sometimes, you're forced to make hard decisions that feel uncomfortable or even unfair, but those decisions are essential for the long-term survival and success of your organization. Churchill recognized that, and thank goodness he did, or who knows how the war might have turned out. Not only that: Even now, years later, most people don't remember Auchinleck's name, but Montgomery's is well-known, and historians frequently credit Churchill as being instrumental in ensuring the Allied forces were victorious over the Axis powers.

Recently, I spoke with another business leader who was grappling with the difficult task of letting an employee go. He had delayed the decision for far too long because he didn't want to cause hurt or discomfort. However, he finally took action, sent the necessary email, and—despite his fears—the world didn't fall apart. In fact, his decision likely benefited the employee in the long run, even if that wasn't immediately clear.

This is the reality of leadership. You have to prioritize doing what's right for everyone who relies on you, even when it's uncomfortable. Leadership often demands tough decisions, and as much as you may care (and *should* care) about the people involved, avoiding those decisions only prolongs the suffering. Success in business requires tackling difficult issues directly. You can't afford to shy away from the hard calls. On the contrary, those are the moments that define your leadership.

I won't sugarcoat it: It's never easy. But embracing discomfort and pushing through it is going to be part of the journey. If you have the determination to face challenges head-on, you'll be far better positioned for success.

FOUR

THE CORNERSTONES OF SUCCESS

ONE OF THE MOST IMPORTANT LESSONS I LEARNED in the printing business was that I couldn't do everything myself. This realization came during a pivotal time. Like many business owners, I had been trying to manage everything—overseeing daily operations, handling decision-making, and juggling responsibilities—and it left me constantly running on empty.

Eventually, the weight became too much, and I reached a breaking point. It was then that I knew I needed to bring in help. It became clear that if I wanted to scale the business, I had to delegate some of the work. More importantly, I needed to build systems and processes that didn't rely solely on what was in my head. That realization was a game changer for me. My father, unfortunately, took the opposite approach—he was accustomed to and intent on controlling every detail. This difference in mindset contributed to a lot of the tension between us, but I knew that if we were going to grow, we had to change the way things were done.

That period of my career taught me the importance of building sustainable processes and systems, not only for the sake of my sanity but for the survival of the business itself. Getting everything out of my father's head and onto paper was no easy task. Without a mentor guiding me, much of what I did was driven by a combination of instinct and studying the industry. I've always been a keen observer, and I believe that trait is critical for anyone starting out in business. You have to pay attention, observe what works and what doesn't, and learn from the experiences of others. In truth, no business system on earth is entirely new. In fact, every business system out there is just a modification of what has already been figured out by somebody else, somewhere else. So just listen, observe, and take note of your surroundings. I think if you do, you'll find the solutions you need are already in existence, either within your industry or (more likely) outside it.

Along with observation and instinct, you have to work hard, of course. But make no mistake: As essential as hard work is, it's not enough on its own. You have to work smart. Many fledgling entrepreneurs believe they can simply outwork their problems, but the truth is you can't outwork poor decisions or inefficiencies. You need to recognize when something isn't working, take a step back, and approach it from a different angle. Just like when I played high school football, using an identical attack angle with every play eventually stopped working as the offensive line figured out what I was doing. Repeating the same actions will only yield the same results.

The lessons of **delegation**, **observation**, and **working smart** have become some of the cornerstones of my approach to business. Yes, you have to meet problems head-on, but that doesn't mean you can always muscle through every challenge. Sometimes, you need to step back, reassess, and find a better path forward.

TAKING CARE OF PEOPLE

Those three lessons are crucial. But every strong structure is built on *four* solid cornerstones, and for me, the fourth one is **compassion**.

I'm a voracious reader, always trying to learn new things, but in my early days in business, I didn't have much time to actually sit down with a book. Back then, digital content wasn't an option, and we didn't have Audible. What I did have were books on tape. Yep, good ol' cassette tapes. Earl Nightingale's series, in particular, played a key role in shaping my thinking as a budding entrepreneur. He took many of Napoleon Hill's ideas and turned them into practical lessons that I could not only easily grasp but also apply immediately.

I remember buying a course consisting of twelve of Nightingale's tapes, and they became my constant companion on my daily commutes. His voice became like a mentor, and the lesson that stuck with me most was simple but powerful: **You can have everything you want if you help enough other people get what they want.**

If you focus on serving others—whether your customers or your team—the success you're seeking will naturally follow. It's a universal truth: When you help others achieve their goals, your own success becomes an undeniable byproduct. Ironically, I probably learned more from those tapes than from my father, even though he was undoubtedly trying to teach me similar things.

In business, taking care of your employees is just as important, if not more so, than taking care of your customers. Customers come and go, but your team is the backbone of your business.

In the high-intensity, high-stress environment of the printing industry, I saw my employees every single day. It didn't take long to realize that if I didn't show them genuine concern and compassion, the business would suffer.

You don't need to be best friends with your employees or spend time together outside of work, but you do need to show them that they matter. When you build mutual respect and demonstrate that you have their backs, they'll go the extra mile for you. This creates a culture of loyalty where no one wants to let the team down. It also reduces stress and turnover and boosts the overall quality of work.

There are lots of ways to do this. For example, when dealing with clients, I always kept my team's physical capacity in mind. If a project couldn't be delivered by Thursday but could be completed by Friday, I'd be up front with the client. I wasn't about to overcommit just to earn an extra dollar if it meant burning out my team. Constantly pushing people beyond their limits for profit is unsustainable. Eventually, employees will start to feel exploited, and once their trust is broken, it's incredibly hard to repair.

The lesson is straightforward: *When you take care of your people, they'll take care of your business.* Of course, achieving this requires balance. You need to know when to push for results and when to pull back, all while keeping your long-term goals in mind. A workplace culture grounded in mutual respect, compassion, and understanding fosters a team that's genuinely invested in their work, which inevitably elevates the quality of what you deliver to customers.

When I hear about trends like "quiet quitting" or disengaged employees, I can't help but reflect on how these problems might be avoided if more businesses adopted this simple philosophy of service. Throughout my career, I've worked for bosses who showed no interest in me as a person or in the well-being of my family, and that indifference wore me down. Time and again, I've seen managers who only focus on the numbers and utterly ignore the individuals behind the work. This is a leadership failure that has long-tail negative impacts.

My father wasn't like that, but in most of my other roles, I felt like just another cog in the machine. Those experiences solidified my commitment to lead differently. I came to understand that when you treat people with dignity and create a supportive environment, they not only work harder but also take pride in the success of the business. They take emotional ownership, and your business becomes *their* business too.

When my father and I sold Cantrell Graphics in 1988, my then-wife was expecting my oldest daughter. Remember, I departed the acquiring firm a few months after the sale, so I found myself in a race against time to land a new job. Driven by that sense of urgency, I accepted a role as a copy center manager for a national office supply chain. The experience was a disaster. The pay was low, and the management style was toxic. They had zero regard for the fact that I had outside responsibilities, like attending birthing classes with my wife. I was expected to work eighty-hour weeks with no exceptions.

After just four or five months, I left for a position as Sales Manager at R&S Printing, a local firm. However, things went from bad to worse. The company was caught up in the turmoil of the leveraged buyout era. The new owner, who had zero background in commercial printing, was intent on slashing prices and driving volume in the hope of capturing massive market share. His mantra, "We'll make it up on volume," was laughable in an industry with high fixed costs like paper, ink, and capital equipment. Pricing jobs at ninety percent of cost and scaling up only accelerated the losses. This was a catastrophic mistake by someone who had zero operational knowledge and had wormed their way into a key leadership role.

As expected, the strategy failed, and the bank shut down the business. I'll never forget the day we were told to gather our belongings because the doors would be locked the next morning. With a newborn at home, it was a gut-wrenching moment. But it also highlighted the lesson I shared with you earlier: Hard work alone isn't enough. You have to understand how a business operates and, more importantly, care about the people who make it run. If you don't, even your best efforts are doomed to collapse.

PREDISPOSED IS *NOT* PREDETERMINED

Genes, environment, or luck may influence success, but they're only part of the equation. None of them can claim full (or even primary) responsibility for where we end up. At most, they can *predispose* us for certain outcomes, but they don't *predetermine* them. That's one of the biggest issues in society today: too often, people believe that a certain background, personality trait, or family situation automatically sets a ceiling on what they can achieve. But the truth is, success is deeply rooted in what we *choose* to focus on. Our personalities shape our interests, and those interests in turn guide our pursuits, which can amplify our success. Maybe you've heard people explain this phenomenon by saying *what you focus on multiplies*. Well, as simple as it sounds, it's true—and in fact, it's the simplicity of this concept that makes it powerful.

Let me give you a personal example. My own father had every excuse not to succeed. He was a tenth-grade dropout. Growing up, he was surrounded by challenges—the loss of his father when he was just thirteen, limited education, few career prospects. But my father made the *choice* to not allow those predispositions to determine his future. Even when his life could've taken him down a bad path, he eventually put his faith in Christ and turned things around in his thirties. That choice changed everything, both for him personally and for his legacy.

You already know that I inherited some of his independent spirit, especially in my youth, and it could've easily derailed me too. Those same attitudes that might have led me off-track became strengths once I learned to channel them. Instead of letting my energy pull me away from my goals, I redirected it. I chose to focus on the areas where my rebelliousness, my stubbornness, and my drive to do things differently worked in my favor.

That's a key concept I hope every entrepreneur understands: the very qualities that might seem like weaknesses can be powerful strengths if we apply them wisely. It's a page out of Sun Tzu's teachings—understanding that your so-called weaknesses are actually unique strengths when applied in the right context. And once you realize that, those predispositions lose their hold over you. They only become limitations if you *allow* them to be.

Too often, we let external factors serve as excuses. I've heard people say, "Well, I'm a woman, so men aren't going to take me seriously," or, "Well, I wasn't born with a silver spoon in my mouth like that person was, so no wonder they're further along than me." But those are just excuses, and they only hold true if you *believe* them. Show up, present yourself with confidence, and you'll often find the world responds to you differently than you might expect. Ultimately, those predispositions, whether they're based on circumstances, personality traits, or external expectations, are irrelevant unless you make them relevant. The real power lies in knowing you have the choice to turn those predispositions into strengths.

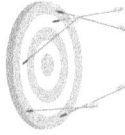

FIVE

READ THE WARNING SIGNS

FTER THESE EARLY CHALLENGES IN MY CAREER, I joined a company called Lellyett & Rogers, which is still thriving today. Initially, I focused on selling print services through my network and aligning clients with the right products. About six years in, I was asked to take on the role of general manager. Essentially, there were the two owners, and everyone else in the company reported to me. While the title might sound lofty, the plant wasn't particularly large at the time—it had about ten employees and generated around $1.5 million in sales annually (equivalent to about $3.5 million in today's money). By the time I left the company for the real estate industry seven years later, we had grown the business to nearly $11 million in annual revenue and 52 employees.

As rewarding as that growth was, I reached a point where I wanted more. I needed more. The two owners, however, weren't planning to step aside any time soon, and there were clearly no opportunities for equity. It was then I truly understood the reality of a glass ceiling in the business world, regardless of gender. I was helping them build a highly profitable business, but the rewards I sought were never going to materialize. I knew it was time to move on.

That realization came about the time I turned forty, which proved to be a pivotal year in my life. After a long downward spiral, my marriage had ended in divorce several months before. Within a year, I married my teenage sweetheart, and shortly after that, I left the printing world for an entirely different industry. It was a period of profound transformation—truly a "go big or go home" moment on every front.

I've always had a talent for sensing when situations are no longer viable, but in early life, I didn't always act on those instincts quickly enough. Many times, I stayed too long, whether in companies, roles, or even relationships, hoping I could turn things around. That impulse to fix problems is a core part of who I am, and while it can be a strength, it's also a potential liability. The danger of that mindset is that it can cloud your judgment and cause you to miss warning signs. Sometimes, you have to pivot sooner rather than later. Today, I make decisions with more agility. I have learned to quickly discern if something isn't working and whether or not I can actually fix it. If not, I move on swiftly. Pain is a powerful educator, and the slower you move, the more it hurts.

The printing industry has a "use you up and throw you away" mentality that I just couldn't ever subscribe to. It is a business where every day is a dogfight, from start to finish. Market share comes from eviscerating the competition on price, which means intense and unending scrutiny on managing every single expense. In fact, a company is considered an "industry leader" if they manage to retain a 3% net profit at the end of the year, with the average being just half that amount. I saw colleagues in their fifties who were self-medicating, chain-smoking alcoholics, burnt out from years of relentless pressure. I knew I didn't want to end up as an old printing salesman—that would have been my version of purgatory.

So, at forty, I decided to fully change course before I became another casualty of the industry. I started exploring the idea of transitioning into real estate as a full-time career. I've always been good at carpentry and repairs, so it seemed like a natural fit. As early as the late '80s, I began a sideline business purchasing properties, renovating them, and then selling them a year or so later for a profit.

In the beginning of dabbling in real estate, my then-wife and I would actually move into the houses I was working on. Eventually, I stopped moving us around and shifted to working on the houses during nights and weekends. By 1998, I had two rather strong parallel occupations: commercial printing during the day, and rehabbing houses in my spare time. I was working toward a clear goal—grow the real estate side to a point where I could leave the printing business altogether.

Eventually, I did. The house-flipping business took off, which enabled me to finally walk away from the printing industry. It was a major breakthrough, both personally and professionally. But the transition was far from easy. My first wife was never on board with any type of career switch and especially not any type of entrepreneurial venture. She came from a blue-collar Chicago family with a straightforward mindset: Stick to a stable job until you retire, period. However, that approach simply didn't align with who I am. In truth, our entire marriage was never in alignment, yet I did my best to make it work.

It's the same in life as it is in business: It's always better to acknowledge warning signs and act proactively, rather than waiting for problems to escalate. Ignoring reality only prolongs the inevitable and makes the final outcome even more difficult.

In my career, paying attention to the warning signs led me to transition from the printing business to real estate. In my personal life, it guided me out of an unhappy, misaligned marriage and into a healthier, more fulfilling one with my beautiful wife, Amanda.

When Amanda and I married, I was still balancing my career in commercial printing with a budding real estate rehab business on the side. It was Amanda who first recognized just how desperately toxic the environment at my printing job had become. One day, she sat me down and basically said, "You've got to do something different because this job is going to kill you, and it's going to kill us." And she was right. I was working under two extremely negative men in a soul-draining industry, and it was taking a huge toll on me and our family.

Fortunately, my side projects in real estate had gained enough momentum to provide an income, so I made the leap and left the printing world behind to focus on real estate full-time. I obtained my real estate license, and the rest, as they say, is history.

Ignoring a partner's intuition is, in my view, one of the gravest mistakes a person can make. My darling wife saw things I couldn't, and I'm grateful every day that I listened to her. Her insight, combined with my faith, resilience, determination, and commitment to family, has been the foundation of everything I've accomplished.

BURN THE BOATS

Now, to be clear, leaving a six-figure job wasn't easy, nor could I do it on a whim. It required deliberate planning and preparation (note: if you want to succeed, you must *always* have a plan). I set aside $50,000 (a sum that would be equivalent to about $150,000 today) as a financial cushion. That amount was key; it was enough to pay for our needs for an entire year. Even though I had been rehabbing properties and had several lined up to sell, I felt an obligation to ensure that my family had a solid safety net. I also established a clear financial goal: My first year in real estate had to surpass my final year in printing. And it did.

During the transition, however, there was a period in which things weren't progressing as quickly with the rehabs as I'd hoped. For six months, I returned part-time to a printing job to stabilize my income. While it was a practical move, it ultimately held me back. Eventually, I realized I needed to adopt a "burn the boats" mentality and cut ties with the printing world for good. That decision made all the difference. When you keep an easy escape route open, it becomes far too tempting to use it the moment things get difficult—that's human nature. But when you remove the safety net and commit fully, that's when real progress happens. Once I severed all ties to my former industry, everything began to click into place. From that point on, there was no looking back.

At the same time, having clear, measurable goals—knowing exactly what I was aiming for—kept me focused and motivated. During any major career or life change, there will always be obstacles, excuses, and moments of doubt. But if your goals are crystal clear, they become a guiding force that pulls you through the tough times.

Like many entrepreneurs, I've learned that I thrive when the pressure is high, when the stakes are elevated—when the "barbarians are at the gate." And it's no surprise. High-stress situations have a way of catalyzing growth and innovation. History is full of examples where periods of intense pressure led to significant innovations or breakthroughs. Many of the greatest advancements in medicine, for example, were born out of the necessity and urgency of war. Penicillin was developed during World War II and transformed the treatment of bacterial infections. Anesthesia emerged during the Civil War to manage pain from battlefield surgeries. Plastic surgery was pioneered in response to the disfiguring wounds of World War I. Chemotherapy originated from research on chemical warfare agents. These innovations didn't happen because everything was calm and orderly.

On the contrary, they emerged because the stakes were high and failure wasn't an option.

The same principle applies to business. When the environment around you is chaotic and every option seems fraught with risk, that's when you're *forced* to find new ways forward. Some people buckle under that pressure, but others thrive. I've always been able to perform at my best in these moments of crisis. Not everyone does, but I believe that if more entrepreneurs could embrace this mindset—if they could learn to push through discomfort instead of retreating—they'd achieve far more than they ever thought possible.

Fear is a powerful motivator, but it cuts both ways. There's the fear of failure, which is easy to recognize. But then there's also the fear of success, which can be even more insidious. I think that fear comes from the trepidation people feel about being in uncharted territory. It's like Wile E. Coyote chasing the Road Runner off the cliff—he's fine until he looks down and panics. But once you experience that first breakthrough, once you get a taste of real success, everything changes. You begin actively seeking out success, eliminating any barriers that stand in the way of your progress. At that point, fear no longer paralyzes because you've harnessed it to propel you forward.

Sometimes, the fear of success comes from a reluctance to stand out. It may sound crude, but humans, by nature, aren't so different from chickens in a coop. When one bird acts differently—say, because it's wounded—the rest instinctively will turn on it and peck at it until they kill it. People can behave in much the same way. The moment you stand out, attempt to break free from the status quo, or aim higher, there's a collective effort to pull you back down. It's inevitable, so be prepared for the attacks of the naysayers. Decide in advance how you'll respond, because your reaction to that resistance will shape your trajectory.

If you allow others to convince you to back down, you've already lost. But if you adopt a mindset of resilience—something like, "Watch me do this twice, and take notes while you're at it"—you set the stage for something extraordinary. That's been another one of my guiding principles: *Never let other people define your limits*. Burn the boats, eliminate the fallback plan, and push forward relentlessly. You might need to strategically pivot, but quitting should never be part of the equation.

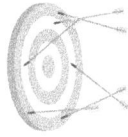

SIX

BREAKING THE CYCLE OF NEGATIVITY

O UR OWN BAD HABITS AND NEGATIVE THINKING patterns can easily become the greatest hindrances to our success, both in life and in business. When things don't go our way—whether it's losing a client, missing out on an opportunity, or having a slow month—we can fall into a downward spiral of self-pity and frustration. This response only magnifies the problem and creates a self-fulfilling cycle of stagnation and decline.

You absolutely must break these cycles of negativity if you want to find success. One of the most powerful lessons I've learned in this area comes from Tony Robbins. Tony recommends using a physical trigger to snap yourself out of a negative state. The trigger can be as simple as clapping your hands very hard one time at the instant you feel that familiar, negative mindset creeping in. That sudden, sharp physical action disrupts the conditioned thought response and forces a mental reset. It may seem trivial, but it is critical to interrupt the mental pattern at the moment of stimulus and create a space for a better, more intentional response.

During my years in the printing business, I started taking early morning walks, sometimes starting as early as 4:30 AM, and using that time to reset my thinking. There I'd be, walking in the dark with my headphones on, listening to Tony Robbins, clapping my hands every hundred yards or so to break out of my own negative thought patterns while repeating such mantras as "Day by day, in every way, I'm getting better and better." I did it over and over again. I'm sure the neighbors thought I was crazy, but it worked. This physical act altered the familiar pattern, shifting my mindset and helping me approach challenges from a place of confidence and clarity instead of frustration or defeat. My goal was to break the pattern and choose a better path, even when external circumstances (and sometimes the people around me) were trying to pull me back down.

For a long time, I didn't even realize how deeply I had internalized the negativity of my environment. It's easy to fall into that trap when everyone around you is stuck in the same mindset. One day, though, I had a moment of clarity—I was letting the negativity of the people around me dictate my life. As soon as I made the conscious decision to stop feeding into those thoughts, things began to change. I started closing more deals and attracting better clients. It was a complete turnaround, and it all began with a mental shift.

The energy you project has a magnetic effect. It is a principle of the universe that like forces attract each other, and opposite forces repel each other. That means positivity attracts positive outcomes, while negativity pulls negative experiences your way. If you're caught in a negative mindset, you'll eventually find yourself on a steep decline. But the inverse is also true. When you proactively reject negative thinking, you open the door to new opportunities and better results.

The key is finding a strategy that works for you to disrupt the pattern. It doesn't have to be a pre-dawn walk. Maybe it's a quick workout, playing with your pets, taking a short drive—anything that jolts you out of that mental rut and allows you to return with a fresh perspective. Believe me when I say that taking the time to do this allows you to create the mental and physical space necessary to reset your mind and approach challenges more effectively.

This approach is especially important for entrepreneurs. According to the US Bureau of Labor Statistics, 23.2 percent of private sector businesses in the US fail within the first year, and almost half of them don't last five years. Often, this isn't because the business model is flawed, but because the founders get trapped in their own negative mindset. They become reactive, stop investing in their own growth, and fall into the habit of hosting pity parties for themselves—something Zig Zigler called "stinking thinking" and my father always warned me against.

Successful entrepreneurs learn to master the gap between stimulus and response. They recognize the moment negativity starts to creep in and disrupt it before it takes root. They find ways to snap out of self-defeating mindsets and return to solving problems with renewed focus and energy. That ability to reset and realign, rather than wallow or retreat, often makes the difference between a business that crumbles and one that thrives.

A major part of maintaining this mental discipline is controlling what you allow into your mind. Consuming a steady diet of negative news and doom-and-gloom media predictions can trigger a physical response that weighs you down for days. If you start your day inundated by headlines forecasting disaster, your subconscious internalizes that garbage, and it impacts your mood, your decisions, and your productivity. It is absolutely imperative that you guard your mental space. Choose to engage with content that inspires growth, such as devotionals on business lessons of the Bible, books on thought leadership, or working on developing new skills. By filling your mind with positivity and proactive thinking, you create a buffer against the doom and gloom that often derails others. The reality is, most of those dramatic news stories have little to no direct impact on your life or business anyway. Stop the negativity before it takes root, and you'll be less likely to need drastic course corrections later on.

Think of this as mental strength conditioning. Training your mind to interrupt negativity and refocus may be gradual and incremental at first. It requires time and repetition to build new habits. Like muscle strength training, you must stick with it to see results. However, each time you consciously redirect your focus, you strengthen your mental foundation and make it easier to stay resilient when faced with challenges.

Looking back, I sometimes wish I had developed this discipline earlier in my career. But the journey of learning to master my mindset has brought me to where I am today. Now, these cycle-breaking habits are automatic. I am able to minimize negativity almost instinctively, especially during high-risk decisions or ambitious pursuits.

By learning how to take control of your mindset, you can also regain the power to consciously choose your path instead of letting fear or negativity dictate your choices.

NEVER LOSE SIGHT OF YOUR PIPELINE

When I first made the move into primarily selling real estate, I was mostly working with other rehabbers to source properties and advise on renovations. For a time, that model worked. My first January was outstanding. February was even better, with negotiations, inspections, and six closings back to back. But then March arrived, and I was blindsided by a harsh reality: My pipeline had run dry.

Suddenly, I was staring into a void. It was a tough lesson, but an important one: *Never lose sight of your pipeline.* Regardless of what industry you are in, no matter how busy you are, always carve out time to cultivate future business. It's easy for new entrepreneurs to get swept up by short-term success and think, "I'm killing it! I'm going to make $50,000 this month." But when that momentum fades and the deals slow down, reality quickly sets in. Without a steady flow of prospects, you're left scrambling to cover even the basics.

This experience taught me that success isn't just about avoiding negativity; it's about cultivating a mindset that prioritizes taking consistent, *proactive* action to build a sustainable business. I'm not saying this to sound preachy or cliché. These are lessons I learned firsthand. I've thrown my own pity parties, felt sorry for myself, and wallowed in frustration, but I've *also* learned to tell myself, "Okay, Phillip, you can feel bad for a moment, but then get your butt in gear and keep moving."

This requires a delicate balance of celebrating short-term wins while maintaining focus on long-term goals. Celebrate the win of the individual battles, but never lose sight of the fact that your mission is to win the entire war. The key is to keep your focus on what's next: prospecting, building relationships, and staying disciplined with daily habits that ensure the pipeline is always full. Never get so absorbed in the immediate results that you neglect to build for future success. In business, it's not just about reaching the top, but making sure you put in the work necessary to stay there.

TAKE CARE OF YOURSELF

Finally, amid the relentless demands of building and growing a business, you have to find ways to prioritize self-care. Over the years, I've come to realize just how important it is to incorporate intentional practices that counterbalance the chaos of work and daily life.

One practice that has been transformative for me is sensory deprivation, or isolation tank floats. Picture yourself lying in a tank with 15 inches of warm, heavily salt-infused water, ears plugged, entirely separated from the outside world. There's no sound, no light, just a sensation of floating in space with zero gravitational pressure. It's a unique experience that allows the mind to detach and reset. After each session, I feel rejuvenated for days. The moment I step out of the tank, I feel as though weeks of tension have been erased, replaced by a sense of clarity and peace.

I usually begin these floats by mentally transporting myself to Jordan Pond in Acadia National Park. If you've never been, it's a beautiful lake with a glass-like surface, surrounded by dense forest and majestic mountains. In my mind, I walk around the lake's perimeter, shedding layers of stress with each lap, almost as if I'm rebuilding myself piece by piece and step by step in this place of solitude and tranquility.

Your mind is your most powerful asset. It's the cornerstone of your well-being, productivity, and resilience. I've seen firsthand how unchecked stress can erode your health. Indeed, it's often the silent trigger behind anxiety, anger, and, in extreme cases, more severe conditions like cardiovascular disease or even cancer.

Not long ago, I was talking to another entrepreneur who was going through this firsthand. The compounded stress of work and the grief of losing a family member took a toll on her immune system and left her physically drained and emotionally depleted. She ended up getting seriously ill. When we talked about it, our conversation was a stark reminder of how profoundly our mindset can influence our physical health.

During our conversation, I reminded her—as I'm reminding you—how important it is to pause, acknowledge when you've hit your limit, and allow yourself time to recover. Yes, as a business owner, often you have to be the one pushing the hardest, but it's just as important to know when to step back and regroup. Recognize those moments of vulnerability and respect your body's need for restoration, because self-care is just as critical to long-term success as resilience, grit, and perseverance.

So, take time to care for yourself, release the stress, and find places (both physical and mental) where you can recharge. Remember, success isn't just about endurance; it's about sustaining yourself for the journey ahead. Finding success in business isn't one constant sprint. It is a marathon. Find your spaces of calm and healing, and use them to fortify your mind and body for the challenges that will inevitably come.

SEVEN

WORK HARD, WORK SMART

MINDSET IS IMPORTANT, BUT I ABSOLUTELY believe that many new businesses also fail for another reason: They didn't plan or manage their cash flow properly. For me, my goal in my first year of rehabbing homes was simple: to exceed the income I made in my last year in commercial printing. I'm a big believer in setting SMART goals—*specific*, *measurable*, *achievable*, *relevant*, and *time-bound*. So I wrote my goal down, and by the end of the year, guess what? I had exceeded my previous annual income by $5,000.

That difference wasn't a huge sum, but the fact that I had accomplished it was validation that I was on the right track. To this day, I directly attribute this achievement to having written goals. If you don't write down your goals, they're just wishes. But if you define them, work toward them, and track your progress, you'll be amazed at what you can achieve. This concept is important, so let me say it clearly: *An unwritten goal is nothing but a wish.*

I figured if I could match the income I was making in my previous career, then I would know I had something sustainable. I think that's a valid way to approach any entrepreneurial venture. If you can at least match your current income, then the business has legs. If you can't, it's time to reassess and figure out a new plan—whether that means going back to your old industry or finding another job.

I've had conversations with other entrepreneurs who share their revenue goals with me. They increase their goals every year, and like me, they usually manage to hit them. Sometimes it's really close, but they hit the target. Then there are others who say, "I'm just trying to make enough to get by." That mindset always puzzles me. "Enough to get by" is not a goal. It's vague and intangible—how do you even know what "enough" is? And how can you aim for something if you don't define it?

Honestly, I think "getting by" isn't a goal at all—it's an excuse. An excuse for when failure comes. And anytime you give yourself permission to fail, guess what happens? Yep. You fail. I don't get it...but then again, as you probably realize by now, I've never been the type of person to allow myself that option.

PROVING MYSELF RIGHT

Because I set concrete goals, manage my cash flow, and plan well, I am able to succeed where many others expect me to fail. For example, when I walked into my boss's office on January 2nd to resign from my role as a general manager in the printing business, my boss laughed and said, "You can't leave here. You'll never survive on your own. Besides, you're the f-ing general manager!"

But I was dead set on leaving, so I told him, "I'm giving you ninety days to find a replacement. I'm leaving April 1st, whether you're ready or not."

He scoffed at the idea, but as the weeks went by and they still hadn't hired anyone, I kept reminding them—at sixty days, then forty-five days, and then at thirty—that this train *was* leaving the station. Eventually, they brought someone in, and I began training my replacement. That poor fellow got a full-bore crash course in running a 50,000-square-foot printing plant over a twenty-five-day period. Surely he resented me for that aborted training, but I wasn't the one who had put him in that predicament.

Even after I made it clear I was departing, my boss didn't believe I'd make it. He'd shake his head and say to me, "You won't last out there. You'll be back in here looking for a job soon."

He might've been joking, but I didn't take it that way. I took it as a challenge, just as I had so many times in the past, saying to myself "Oh yeah? Well, watch this, big boy." And even after I left, many of the employees would reach out to tell me they were waiting for me to "come to my senses" and return. Their mental state held them so tightly captive that they couldn't imagine me leaving and succeeding outside the printing business. But for me, their doubts were just more fuel to keep pushing me forward. Every bit of skepticism I encountered only made me more determined.

Exactly twelve months after I left, I went back to visit the people in the plant. I had a lot of respect for the workers there, and I wanted to catch up. When my old boss saw me, he sauntered over, acting casual. I'm sure he fully expected that I was there to ask for my old job back. Instead, I told him, "You said I wouldn't make it. Well, I just want you to know that I've exceeded my income from when I was here, and I've done it in just one year." Then, with a cheery smile, I added, "Have a nice day."

He was completely dumbfounded, and weakly muttered, "Congrats."

I'll admit, that moment felt good. I'm not one to revel in revenge, but it was satisfying to set the record straight. It was never about proving him wrong—it was about proving *to myself* that I could succeed on my own terms. But as you know by now, my success didn't happen accidentally. I had the drive and determination to do whatever I needed to do to succeed.

I meet so many people who lack that drive, that fire in the belly, and it frustrates me. I try to wake people up, to light that spark, but I know I can't reach everyone. It's an uphill battle: As a society, we're trained from a young age to follow orders. In elementary school, we're taught to get in line, stay in line, keep quiet, and ask for permission to do the simplest things. That conditioning continues into adulthood, and it governs our lives unless we choose to break the cycle.

For me, that fire was ignited by my circumstances growing up. I developed a "lead, follow, or get the hell out of my way" mentality. I was coming through, and nothing was going to stop me. That's how I've approached every challenge in life, and it's a mindset I've carried into my business ventures. It helped me keep moving forward even when other people— including many people I like and trust—were skeptical of my chances.

Look, you don't have to prove anything to anyone else. Prove it to yourself. Let the fire burn within you as you press on to achieve the goals you've set for yourself. Don't let the doubts of even well-intentioned people determine *your* future.

Having said that, remember that victory isn't going to be handed to you on a silver platter. Your drive will keep you going, but it's not enough, by itself, to ensure success. You have to combine that attitude with careful planning, hard work, and consistency.

IT'S A MARATHON, NOT A SPRINT

Many people have a romanticized idea of entrepreneurship that has been shaped by stories about people like Bill Gates, Steve Jobs, and Jeff Bezos—legendary founders who started in garages and built massive empires. But the reality is, none of these people achieved success easily, accidentally, *or* overnight.

Sure, Amazon started in a garage, but look more closely at Bezos's story. He was working on Wall Street when he decided to load up his car and head to Washington state to start Amazon. He started with very little savings, and everyone told him he couldn't do it—that he was throwing away his career. But he had enough tenacity, resilience, and belief in his model and himself to push through all that noise. In his case, it took twelve long years before turning the first profit.

That's what entrepreneurship really boils down to: having faith in what you're doing, working hard to build the skill set you need to succeed, and then *grinding it out*. It's not glamorous, and it's not about overnight success. Most people get caught up in the fictitious fantasy of rapid glory, and then become disillusioned when reality doesn't match up to their dreams. They need a hard dose of reality—something to snap them out of fantasyland and get them focused on the real work.

As I always say, **you have to get comfortable with the boring**. Success isn't about excitement and sudden glory; it's about the daily grind. It's about acknowledging that there are plenty of tasks you may not want to do, but they need to get done, and you're the one who has to do them—at least at this stage of your business. It's about showing up, day in and day out, and doing the hard things consistently and over a long period of time. It's not about becoming an overnight success, either—frankly, that idea is a myth. The reality is more like "overnight success after a lot of years of damn hard work."

STEADY PROGRESS WINS

Successful businesses are built on processes, not personalities. Yes, you need to know how to interact with people, especially if you're in sales. But even a great personality will only take you so far. The real key is having solid procedures and systems in place. It's about doing the same thing day in and day out, and refining it as you go. That's how the multi-year "overnight" success story happens—through grit, persistence, and the willingness to do the boring, repetitive tasks most people shy away from.

In his book *Great By Choice*, Jim Collins talks about the "Twenty-Mile March," and it's a perfect analogy for this. This is a greatly abbreviated version, but it's the story of two explorers who sought to be the first to plant their country's flag at the South Pole. One of them had a clear strategy: March twenty miles every day, no matter the conditions. If it was snowing and miserable, he did twenty miles. If it was sunny and clear, he still only did twenty miles. He stuck to his consistent, methodical plan, no matter what.

The other explorer took a different approach. When the weather was good, he would sprint, covering as much ground as possible—sometimes forty miles in a day. But when the weather was bad, he'd hunker down and rest. His journey was erratic— some days he'd push hard, other days he'd do almost nothing. Days turned into weeks, weeks turned into months. In the end, he ran out of supplies just five miles from his destination and perished. The first explorer, who stuck to the steady twenty-mile march, was the one who made it to the South Pole—and even more importantly, made it back home again.

Consistency wins. Not the sprints, not the bursts of energy when things are good, not the hunkering down when things are bad. It's the steady, reliable progress—every day—that gets you to your goal. In business, when you can sprint, you shouldn't. Instead, conserve your energy, your capital, and your resources for the long haul. Steady progress builds something that lasts.

Every little adjustment you make, every incremental improvement, compounds over time. At first, it might feel like you're just turning the screw a quarter turn here, a quarter turn there. But before you know it, you've turned the screw all the way around, and you look back to realize how far you've come. That's the beauty of entrepreneurship—it's about doing the work, day after day, and letting those small improvements accumulate into something much bigger over time. If you approach it with that mindset, you'll have the resilience to succeed where others exhaust themselves and give up.

It's easy to get caught up in the idea of rushing toward glory. I've certainly felt that urge myself, even though I know better. We all love the excitement of chasing after swift success. But the problem is, when you rely on sprinting, you eventually hit tough days where the momentum slows, and suddenly you're running on empty. You've depleted all your energy and resources, and you're left feeling drained and unmotivated.

That's why it's so important to shift your mindset from short bursts of energy to long-term endurance. In business, you're in it for the long haul. There's a trend in today's economy where people want to build something fast, sell it, and then jump to the next thing. They do it over and over, riding the wave while it lasts. But for me, *entrepreneurship is about being comfortable in the dirt*. It's about embracing the grit and the grind. In the military, they call it "embracing the suck"—getting comfortable with the grossly uncomfortable tasks. That's how you actually achieve your goals. It's not glamorous, but it's real.

MINOR COURSE CORRECTIONS

Consistency also means you focus on making minor course corrections rather than big, sweeping changes. Minor course corrections can make a tremendous difference over time. Take, for example, the trajectory of an airplane: If you alter the course by even one degree, it creates a 92.2-foot deviation after just one mile. Think that doesn't sound like a lot? Then consider that when you stretch that over a cross-country flight from San Francisco to Washington, DC, you end up a whopping 42.6 miles off course. In other words, you completely miss your target.

Just as with an airplane's course, daily incremental improvements are critical. Let's do some simple math so you can see what I mean. The number 1 raised to the 365th power is still 1. That means zero improvement per day equals zero improvement in a year. However, the number 1.01 raised to the 365th power is 37.8.

In other words, a simple 1 percent daily improvement results in a cumulative *38 percent* improvement in just one year. The math gets even crazier from there. 1.02 raised to the 365th power is 1,377.4. That's an astounding *1,400 percent improvement*—and it's achievable in just one year simply by making a 2 percent change in your daily habits and processes!

None of this is theoretical—it's statistical fact. But too many people go through their lives without realizing the power of small, incremental changes. They sit around and wait for some big, dramatic shift to happen, but the momentous change never comes. That's why so many people look back on their lives with regret; they realize the big change they were always waiting for never happened.

I hope, if you take nothing else from this book, you'll take this lesson to heart. Life is shaped by the small, daily decisions we make, not by a single transformative moment. I spent nineteen years in commercial printing, expecting some breakthrough, and not fully understanding the potential of small adjustments. In reality, it's the one extra call each day, the one extra task, or the one more process you put in place that eventually builds momentum. It's like compound interest. Any financial advisor will tell you the power isn't just in saving money but in how those savings compound over time. The growth comes from the compounding benefit, not just the physical act of saving. The same concept applies to life and business. Unfortunately, most people abandon their efforts long before they reach that tipping point. I was guilty of this myself. But once I saw the impact of minor adjustments, I realized they could yield exponential results over time.

My philosophy now is straightforward: Establish clear processes and make consistent improvements over the long haul. Here at Benchmark, we make minor tweaks as we refine our processes, but we're not focused on big shifts or the next shiny object. Consistent processes lead to repeatable outcomes. When you know what the end result will be if the process is followed, you gain control over your outcomes. And if you're not happy with the outcome? It doesn't take a monumental shift to adjust it—sometimes, a minor tweak is all you need. Think back to that 42.6-mile drift from San Francisco to DC, and then trust that the small course corrections, rather than the drastic overhauls, will make all the difference.

One caveat here: For the minor course corrections to work, everyone has to be aligned. The attitude must be, "We're all pulling in the same direction." Without alignment, you may have people rowing in different directions, which will hinder the progress of the whole boat. If you find someone consistently out of sync, cut them loose. Otherwise, they'll act like an anchor weighing down the whole crew. Everyone has to be on the same page, focused, and rowing forward together for true progress.

HOW TO OBTAIN CONSISTENT RESULTS

I've talked a lot about processes here, so let me take a moment to define what I mean. When I talk about "processes," I mean that a successful business needs clear, standardized steps that everyone can follow to ensure consistent results. Break down large tasks into smaller, manageable pieces and standardize them in order to create a pathway to predictable outcomes. Without this, every day will feel like you're reinventing the wheel, and your business will become entirely dependent on a few select individuals to achieve the desired results.

I saw the value of processes early in my career. When I took over as general manager at Lellyett & Rogers, the workflow was dictated by the machine operators, who would pick up job tickets and often choose tasks based on what they felt most comfortable doing. For example, if a job looked like it could be wrapped up by 4:30, they'd take it, but if it would spill over into the next day, they avoided it to save the hassle of washing up the press and resetting it.

This was highly problematic because harder tasks were often left undone or created an unfair burden on the few individuals unafraid of the more complex jobs. To tackle this, I implemented a scheduling system that changed everything. Using a visual magnet board, I assigned each job a magnet with an insert that detailed the task. I reviewed the magnets every morning and evening with our production superintendent to rebalance the plant workload to meet the deadlines. While this wasn't revolutionary—it was essentially just Stephen Covey's principle of "begin with the end in mind"—it was transformative for the company. For the first time, we had a clear deadline and estimated production times for each workstation, so we knew what needed to happen every day to hit our deadlines. Once this system was in place, productivity tripled. It was a simple yet incredibly effective shift, and it demonstrated the power of process over personality.

I saw a similar need for standardization when I entered the real estate business and founded Benchmark Realty. In this industry, most people who reach leadership positions get there through sales, with little experience in production or operations or even business knowledge in general. Basically, the majority "sell" their way to the leadership role. I wanted to do things differently. So, I took what I'd learned from manufacturing, tweaked it, and applied it to Benchmark—in effect creating a business where processes ruled. I also worked with my team to set up a standardized entry system, compliance system, and accounting system, which ensured that every transaction followed a strict sequence of steps. If a deal closes by noon (and the paperwork has been approved by the compliance department already), agents know they'll be paid by 5:00 PM the same day. Many people couldn't believe this was possible; some thought we were somehow bending the rules. One competitor even told his agents that what we were doing was illegal! But the truth is that simple processes, followed without exception, deliver consistently excellent results.

Let's take transaction file compliance as an example. Each transaction at Benchmark has a checklist that outlines essential steps and categorizes them as mandatory or optional. If anyone tries to sidestep this process, it quickly gets flagged and kicked back to the agent, even if clients remain unaware. We have so many processes like these to keep the ship running smoothly. And it works. Managing 10,000+ closings a year (equaling 20,000+ sets of paperwork when you add the listing-side paperwork to the total) with a small team of two compliance people and three accounting people isn't easy. But with a system like ours, it's doable. And here's the thing: We don't rely on advanced AI or automation; we rely on process structure.

As a business leader, if you skip the foundational work, you will end up in chaos. Every morning, you'll face one frustrating question: "What am I supposed to do today to drive my business forward?" It's too easy to pick the comfortable tasks while leaving the tough ones to pile up, which leads to a backlog, frustrated clients, and disappointed agents. This is where you can rely on the mantra: **reduce everything to its simplest sequence.** Think logically through each step, and you'll arrive at a reliable and repeatable outcome.

Standardizing processes can be painful work because, in some cases, it flies in the face of human nature, but it's necessary. Remember what I wrote earlier about "embracing the suck"? Perfect example here! It forces you to do the tasks you'd rather avoid and pushes you out of your comfort zone. You have to be comfortable being uncomfortable. If you can reach that point emotionally, spiritually, and psychologically, you'll set yourself apart. You already know that most people do everything they can to avoid pain. But just like those early football drills of mine, facing the tough stuff head-on builds resilience and lays the groundwork for lasting success.

CLEAR COMMUNICATION

As you now know, making processes and systems work requires that everyone is aligned and rowing together in the same direction. But you can only get your whole team on the same page if there's clear communication. Because here's the thing: **People don't internalize a message the first time they hear it**—or even the sixth. Communication in business is all about repetition. If you want a message to stick, you need to be willing to say it over and over again, even when you're tired of hearing it yourself. As a leader, you're essentially the "Chief Reminding Officer," responsible for reinforcing who you are as a team, what you do, and why you do it. It's a role that requires patience, consistency, and a willingness to repeat the same message time and again. Some say that "CEO" actually stands for "Chief Email Officer," and I'm not sure I disagree with that.

At times, it feels a bit like raising kids. If you have multiple children, each will come to you with the same question at different times. By the third time you answer it, you may feel exasperated, but for that child, it's the first time they're hearing the answer. Employees are no different. You have to adopt the mentality of "keep saying it, keep saying it, keep saying it." That is the only way to make sure everyone gets the message, and it's the only way to build a consistent culture.

This is sometimes easier said than done. At Benchmark Realty, I got so frustrated with trying to convey our core values that I finally wrote them all down in a document called "*What It Takes to Thrive at Benchmark*." This paper became a touchstone for our full-time employees, clearly outlining our philosophy *and* including a reminder of who our client is (because in any business, it is absolutely critical to understand your clientele). In our model, our client is the *agent*, not the consumer (the consumer is the agent's customer).

This distinction is crucial to our organization's culture. I remind employees regularly about being professional in every interaction with our affiliated agents, despite how frustrating the work can be at times. The agents are the ones who provide our livelihood, pay our bills, and ultimately support our families. I didn't just write the document and distribute it once, either; every eight to twelve months, I bring this paper back into circulation. Every time I do, it's because I've seen the need to remind our people about these simple yet crucial concepts again.

As a leader, it's your job to identify your organization's core values and repeat them until they become second nature for everyone in the company. This is called building your culture. Repeating the message can be tedious, especially for team members who've been around long enough to hear it many times. But for the employee who's been here thirty, ninety, or even 120 days, it may be the first time they're truly hearing and understanding it. Even though your guidelines may be available on the company portal and in your manuals, some employees don't absorb them until they hear it directly. And if they don't hear it from you, they will fill in the gaps on their own.

When there's a lack of clear communication, people *will* create their own narratives. If something significant happens in a business and the leader doesn't address it directly—explaining what happened and what the response will be—employees will start speculating. They'll piece together explanations based on rumors, assumptions, how a similar situation was handled at their last company, or what they've read elsewhere. And that's when organizational morale goes sideways. The absence of a clear message doesn't result in silence; it results in people creating a story for themselves, and often, it's the wrong one.

Being a leader means controlling that narrative. If you're consistent in your messaging, you build trust. Employees begin to know you, to understand where you're going, and to anticipate your responses. Over time, your message becomes a guiding principle. The team knows they can rely on you to be direct and honest, and that consistency becomes a centering compass for the organization.

If a leader doesn't communicate clearly and often, that void gets filled. If a leader is absent, that void gets filled. If a leader is distracted, the void still gets filled. People need direction, and if they don't get it from you, they'll look elsewhere. To build a successful business, you need to repeat your vision, your values, and your purpose endlessly. Explain your processes clearly and often. Make yourself the "Chief Reminding Officer" of who you are and why you're here, and your people will follow you—because they know exactly where you're going and why.

EIGHT

CAREFUL PLANNING IS CRITICAL

F YOU'RE GOING TO ENDURE AS AN ENTREPRENEUR, you have to find an industry that you're somewhat passionate about. At the very least, you need to enjoy what you're doing on a daily basis. Otherwise, you're wasting your life.

I spent nineteen years in an industry I didn't love because of family expectations, financial pressures, and all the responsibilities that came with having a spouse, kids, and bills. You may face the same thing, and if you do, you know that those things can hold you in place whether you want to be there or not. But staying in a job that doesn't align with you will damage you in the long run. I got out, but it seemed like everyone my age whom I knew in publishing when I left was either a chain-smoker, an alcoholic, or both.

That doesn't mean you have to love your work so much that you would be willing to do it for free. I've occasionally heard someone say, "I would do this job even if they weren't paying me to do it." I don't believe that's necessary (or even true in most cases). But you do need to find joy in the small things and the incremental progress. You need to be okay with the daily grind and find satisfaction in the journey, in contributing toward something greater than yourself.

At the same time, I think you also need to find joy in watching others succeed alongside you. For example, in the real estate business, where agents get paid on commission, I get immense satisfaction when I hand an agent a check for $150,000 because they've just closed a $5 or $6 million deal. In our model, they keep almost all of their commission except for a small fee—at most, just $634. That's so rewarding for me. Especially considering that under a traditional model, that agent would have paid the company about $30,000 out of their commission. Netting only 80% of what they had worked so hard for. When you see someone float out of your office with that kind of success, it's hard not to feel proud and very fulfilled.

This is so important that I'm going to make a bold statement: If you don't find joy in helping others succeed, then entrepreneurship may not be for you. You need to ask yourself the hard questions and examine your motives.

If you're not driven by a desire to improve the lives of others, you might be wasting your time—and theirs. It's okay if you find this is not what drives you. Not everyone needs to be an entrepreneur or a leader. This country needs worker bees too. Go get a steady job; there's absolutely no shame in that. But if you're passionate about what you do, find joy in helping others succeed, and you're consistent, then you just might make it—as long as you go all in.

PASSION ISN'T ENOUGH

Now, having said all of that, let me be clear: passion alone isn't enough. Just because you love your industry, business, product, or clients, there are no guarantees that you'll succeed. Beyond finding joy in the journey, you also have to be smart about how you approach and structure your business. Some really happy and hard-working entrepreneurs have failed simply because they weren't careful about how they ran their business.

There's an old carpenter's rule: measure twice, cut once. It's a simple reminder that careful preparation can save you from costly mistakes, and that philosophy has guided much of my real estate work. You can't just blunder ahead in business and hope the chips all fall in the right place. That's a dangerous game that most people lose. Make sure you have the right tools and that you've planned carefully for the road ahead.

However, even with the right tools and preparation, in my experience, the most frustrating part of business isn't the work itself—it's dealing with other people. Rehabbing real estate is a field where you frequently need to rely on others, and that's where the real challenges lie. Sadly, in the rehab investment industry, there are plenty of people who prey on less knowledgeable investors. Some of the so-called "senior investors" in these real estate investor clubs try to offload their bad deals—what we called "dogs"—onto newcomers. It's disappointing and even heartbreaking to see how many people are willing to take advantage of others in this way.

All the passion, joy, and planning in the world won't spare you from bad faith actors, no matter your industry. Now, I've always believed in giving people the benefit of the doubt. I trust people unless they give me a reason not to. So, when I encountered this behavior in real estate, it was a blow to my faith in people. It was especially jarring because I came from the commercial printing industry, where people would undercut each other just for fun, and I foolishly thought this industry was going to be different.

I wanted to do something positive: buy properties, rehabilitate them, get families into homes, make a profit, and do good work. But I quickly discovered that not everyone shared those same interests or values.

What can you do when you run into this? To a certain extent, when you encounter a bad actor in your industry, you just have to move on. However, beyond that, you can adopt my personal mantra: **trust but verify**. In other words, trust people, but make sure to verify everything they tell you. To this day, it drives my wife crazy that I insist on double-checking everything, but it's a habit I've developed for survival in this business. Far too many hard-working entrepreneurs have had the rug pulled out from under them simply because they trusted the wrong people. Over time, I have gotten better at reading people and trusting my instincts when I feel like something is off, and if you start living by this mantra, you'll be able to do so too.

In addition to honing your instincts, refining your expertise can protect you from being taken advantage of. I became an expert in the process of evaluating prospective properties for that very reason. I realized I needed to know my industry, process, and product inside and out so nobody could pull the wool over my eyes. Eventually, I elevated my skill set and refined my process enough that I could walk into a rough house and, in about thirty minutes, determine what was wrong with it and how much it would cost to fix it, no matter what the seller or the listing agent was trying to claim.

From there, I created spreadsheets with formulas to calculate everything. I'd input my estimates, determine the after-repair value, and back out my costs to arrive at the offer price. Again, bearing down on improving my processes, skills, and knowledge became the best protection I could find to shield me from unscrupulous sellers and bad-faith actors in the industry. It's a shame that this level of self-protection is necessary, but you can't afford to be naïve. Too much depends on you getting things right. There is an upside, though: efficiencies and profit will likely grow rapidly out of these necessary processes.

DESIGNING PARTNERSHIPS

All of that said, you can't let a few bad actors prevent you from working with good people. Most entrepreneurs benefit tremendously from finding competent, reliable partners. That can be easier said than done, though—unfortunately, I've found that most people don't handle partnerships well. Many think they do, but they're often mistaken. Indeed, a partnership is one of the most delicate dynamics in business because it goes far beyond a mere financial agreement; it's like a marriage.

For me, partnerships have taught some hard lessons, starting with my father and our decision to sell Cantrell Graphics. At that time, my dad's energy level was starting to dip, while mine, at twenty-something, was in high gear (and rising). The difference in pace and appetite for growth created tension that started spilling over into family gatherings. We faced the reality head-on: We needed to sell the business if we wanted to protect our family bonds.

Even though he assured me it was his choice to work together, part of me always felt guilty for pulling him away from a stable career at a large printing company. After we sold the business, he never quite regained the same level of success. He spent some time working for the acquiring firm, then moved on to a job with the State of Tennessee, helping set up printing plants inside state correctional facilities. But the high-level executive career he'd left behind was gone forever, and that fact is something I think about often with no small touch of sadness.

Later, I learned another hard lesson about partnerships. This time, it was with a title company I set up after Benchmark Realty was well established. Title insurance is essential in real estate because every mortgage lender requires it, so it seemed like a perfect addition to the business. I formed a new LLC and sourced a young attorney, fresh out of law school, who had worked as a processor in the title world. My wife and I met this person, vetted them on paper, and thought they seemed like a solid choice. So, we offered that person a partnership and made them a 50 percent member of the LLC. But the truth is, I probably rushed into it out of eagerness, blinded by the potential monetary gain of integrating title services into our real estate business. It was a classic personal motivation problem: I was doing it for the money instead of doing it to increase our service to others.

As it turned out, I didn't investigate well enough. Over the four-year partnership, I saw signs that worried me, and eventually, I could no longer ignore them. So, after several failed attempts to resolve the conflict, I made the call to end the partnership. That decision quickly turned ugly, we ended up in court, and the rest, as they say, is history (and, unfortunately, it's history I can't really discuss). Suffice to say it was a costly experience, and while I learned a lot, it wasn't a lesson I wanted to repeat. Essentially, my wife and I found out that the old adage "when you go to court, the only real winners are the attorneys arguing the case" is very true.

My point in telling you this: When it comes to partners, choose carefully so you can avoid having to hammer it out in a courtroom.

Later on, I pretty much did the same thing with an LLC I formed to provide mortgage brokerage services to our affiliated agents. It failed for many of the same reasons. While that one did not end up in court, it did end up costing about $340,000 of my own money before I was able to extract myself from it.

Since that fiasco, I've approached partnerships with extreme caution. Today, I only consider joint ventures—financially arranged deals that can be easily dissolved if things go sideways. Unlike a true business partnership, a joint venture is a temporary arrangement for a specific purpose; it doesn't carry the same "married" feeling. If a joint venture partner messes up, I can simply terminate the arrangement. Truthfully, at this stage of my life and career, I'm no longer interested in being "wedded" to anyone in business.

No matter what kind of partnership you engage in, whether legal partners or a joint venture or even something as basic as joining a real estate team, it should *always* start with clear roles, responsibilities, and expectations. A partnership without these boundaries is like a bad marriage—it drags on, consuming your time, energy, and often, your peace of mind. During those four years in the title company partnership, especially the last two and a half, I learned the true cost of a strained relationship. And it's a cost you can't measure in dollars. What's two and a half years of your life worth? The stress and turmoil are exhausting. Partnerships should *never* be entered into lightly. Do your research, talk to a lawyer, and listen to your gut. And remember:

When in doubt, I've found it's better to go it alone than to be weighed down by a bad partnership.

MANAGE YOUR COSTS AND DEBT

While partnerships can be a source of tremendous tension, nothing causes more strain and stress in business than rising costs and mounting debt. In real estate, especially with rehabbing, you don't make your money when you *sell* the house—you make your money when you *buy* it. If you buy a house at the wrong price, there's no saving the deal. You can't add another room or use higher-end finishes to make up for it. If you've overpaid, you're done. That's a lesson every investor has to learn, and it's one I've carried with me throughout my career.

No one sat me down in the beginning and explained how to calculate costs and track expenses. I had to figure it all out on my own. When I started in the business, I followed the advice of a well-known real estate guru at the time, Carlton Sheets. He was a big name in the 1980s, and in my opinion, he was like the grandfather of real estate investment strategies, especially when it came to rehabbing. I read all his books, adopted his tactics, and they worked—at first. But soon enough, everyone else was reading the same books and following the same strategies, which drove up the prices on distressed properties.

Unfortunately, novice investors often overpay for rough properties, and that's where they get into trouble. Remember—if you pay too much up front, no amount of renovations can make up for that mistake. Many inexperienced investors fall into this trap, then end up turning to hard money lenders, who I always felt were rather predatory. They charge exorbitant interest rates—sometimes 11 or 12 percent—when you can get a bank loan all day long for much less. The terms on these loans are quite onerous as well, usually including a balloon payment in 90–120 days. Fail to make that payment, and a dramatic step up in interest rate is automatically triggered. That means the investor has to work fast to flip the house or risk drowning in debt.

That's how I learned that it's crucial to learn how to manage debt. In fact, **the way you handle your debt is critical to the success of your business.** Ideally, you want to use *retained earnings*—money you've saved from previous profits—to pay for expenses. But in many cases, especially when your business is growing quickly, you may have to borrow to keep up with the cash flow demands.

Even at that point, I wasn't keen on partnerships, but I still needed capital, so I developed a strong relationship with a local bank who understood the rehabbing business. The bank and I had a solid arrangement. They charged a slightly higher interest rate than consumer loans at the time, but nothing predatory.

They would send an appraiser to evaluate the property based on its after-repair value (ARV). For example, if the appraiser determined that the property would be worth $150,000 after the repairs, the bank would lend me 80 percent of that value. This meant I had to focus on buying the property at the right price because if the margins were too thin, I'd have to come up with cash from elsewhere.

At the purchase closing table, the bank would provide the funds to buy the property, and as I completed renovations, they'd release additional funds based on the receipts I turned in. Let's say I bought a house for $65,000 with a bank appraisal ARV of $120,000. That gave me about a $31,000 rehab budget, which the bank would release incrementally ($120,000 x 80% = $96,000 - $65,000 = $31,000). If I needed to pay a vendor before submitting a receipt, I'd use a separate source of funding—often a home equity line of credit (HELOC) on my personal residence. But I always made sure to pay back the HELOC the day I sold the rehabbed property. That discipline kept me afloat in the early days.

In 2002, my first year as a full-time rehabber, I netted a personal income of $85,000 flipping houses. I was involved in about twenty-four real estate transactions that year—buying and selling—and I aimed to complete each rehab project within ninety days. From closing the purchase to closing on the sale of the property, I wanted everything done within that tight window. Of course, that meant I had overlapping projects, but that's where my operations background came in handy. It was intense, but it showed me that if you manage your finances carefully and work efficiently, you can make a good profit.

One of the biggest reasons I eventually got my real estate license was to cut out the middleman and have direct access to key market data—both for buying and selling. When you're working with real estate agents, you're at their mercy. They might be working with multiple investors, and whether or not they like you the best on a given day could determine if you get the best deals. By obtaining a license, I gained firm control over the process of both acquiring and disposing of the properties. I could find the deals myself, negotiate better prices, and handle the sale of the rehabbed properties without relying on someone else. It gave me a significant edge in the business and allowed me to operate on my own terms.

Back when I first started the rehab business, there was no such thing as Zillow or Redfin. If you wanted access to the information contained in the MLS (Multiple Listing Service), you had to become a licensed real estate agent. Without that access, you couldn't function efficiently in the business. I was essentially both the contractor and the person responsible for finding the properties. The real estate agent would dig up potential deals, I'd go check them out, figure out how much I could offer, compete with ten or so other investors, and either get the property or move on to the next one. But once I obtained my real estate license, the game changed. No longer did I have to wait for someone to bring me a deal. I could sit down every night, log into the MLS, and see what was available on my own time. I could even set up alerts so when a property with specific criteria hit the MLS, the system would ping me.

One area of town that worked out really well for me was East Nashville. It was a historic area with some beautiful old homes that had been cut up into apartments, and in many cases had fallen into disrepair. I hit that market at just the right time. You could buy a turn-of-the-century house in rough shape for around $60,000, put another $60,000 into renovations, and sell it for $175,000 all day long. Those same houses are worth over a million dollars now. I wish I'd held onto a few of them, but hindsight is 20/20, and anyway, at the time, I had to keep moving forward.

One house I remember well was on Holly Street, just a few doors down from a historic fire hall that dated back to when fire wagons were still pulled by horses. This house was a beautiful architectural structure, but the place had been lived in by a hoarder. I bought it more or less sight unseen. Walking through it, I saw a narrow pathway through each room, with piles of stuff stacked above my head everywhere else in the rooms. It took two thirty-yard dumpsters just to clean out the junk so I could figure out what I was working with.

Once we cleared it out, we didn't find much value in the piles of stuff, but the house had some great original features, like solid brass door handles, twelve-inch baseboards, and ornate crown moldings. It also had four fireplaces, each covered in layers of paint. After stripping all that paint, we uncovered these beautiful, hand-made tiles in different colors on each fireplace front. We restored the fireplaces, rewired the house, replumbed it, and gutted and installed a new kitchen. That house sold so quickly that the contracts were signed before the work was finished.

Restoring houses like that was the most rewarding part of the business. It wasn't just about rehabbing a structure; it was about bringing something tarnished and neglected back to its original beauty. I enjoyed that kind of work, although I also did plenty of foreclosures—brick ranchers that just needed new kitchen cabinets, carpet, and a fresh coat of paint. Those didn't offer as much of a creative challenge, but they were quicker to flip and required less investment. There was less margin, but also less risk and effort.

The older homes were more fun, but I had to learn the hard way when to stop. My wife Amanda, God bless her, would remind me time and time again, "Stop working on the house;

you're not going to live here!" And she was right. It's important to know when to stop pouring resources into a project and just move on.

Just remember: In *every* business, **cash is king**. You can never afford to neglect your cost structure, and you must always understand how to control it. In the beginning, I didn't have those spreadsheets or sophisticated systems in place. I bumbled my way through, closing deals that seemed like they would bring in big money but ultimately lost a lot because, in those early days, I wasn't tracking my expenses well enough.

If someone had told me what I now know—about making sure you get the house at the right price and carefully managing your costs—I probably would've avoided some early mistakes. But sometimes, bumbling through is how you learn in business. Trial and error (especially the error part!) made the importance of cash management painfully clear to me, particularly when I started borrowing money to fund my projects. Debt service is critical. You have to be diligent about managing it, or it'll sink you.

KNOW YOUR CASH POSITION EVERY DAY

If you want to succeed in business, knowing your cash position daily is non-negotiable. Every day, you need to be aware of exactly what's coming in and what's going out. In the printing industry, it was common for companies to survive on stretched accounts payable. They'd string out those payables as long as possible, hoping they'd have the cash to cover them when the time came. But that kind of habit doesn't lead to long-term stability. Instead, it builds a shaky reputation and fosters a false sense of reliability.

In the service industry, we have it simpler in some ways. You don't have raw materials, production timelines, or extended payables cycles, but the principle remains the same: **Control your expenses tightly.** For example, if you're running a one-time event, like an expo, you need to account for all associated costs and revenue within the same month. Otherwise, your financials get skewed—one month looks like a loss, the next like a windfall. In the long run, consistency and clarity are essential.

At Benchmark Realty, we took a unique approach to eliminate accounts receivable altogether. On the first Friday of each month, we pulled our monthly fees directly from agents' bank accounts, and each transaction fee came in right when we handled a commission payout, so we had—and still have—$0.00 outstanding receivables. We also cleared all accounts payable every Friday, ensuring nothing lingered from one month to the next. It was a simple system that kept our financials clean, our cash flow neat, and our P&L straightforward. So long as revenue outpaced expenses each month, we were on track, and that clarity proved invaluable.

The trouble comes when you let things slip. If you think, "I'll just pay this next month," and revenue doesn't materialize as planned, you're suddenly on a slippery slope of robbing Peter to pay Paul, and possibly falling thirty, sixty, or even ninety days behind. The consequences to this kind of approach can snowball fast.

In the printing world and other industries, vendors often offer discounts—say, a 2 percent discount if you pay within ten days (known as "2/10 net 30"). Taking that discount is free money, and when you're buying in bulk, that 2 percent can add up to a lot of free money every month. In my printing companies, we bought entire boxcars of paper, so I always took those discounts; I knew we'd use the paper eventually, so why not capture the savings? But the core lesson is this: **Never rely on accounts payable to finance your operations**. That's a surefire path to bankruptcy, even if you're technically profitable. It's possible to go under by simply outstripping your cash flow.

Remember, in my own career transition, before I left commercial printing to start in real estate, I made sure I had enough cash to live on for a year. Without that buffer, I might not have made it past six months. Cash reserves allow you to weather the inevitable storms that come with starting any new venture.

Growth periods are especially tricky because expenses often outpace revenue at first. Even if sales are climbing and you are profitable, you're investing heavily in expansion, and that cash outflow can create a crunch. This is why private equity or venture capital firms often step in during these stages, providing the cash injection necessary to capture market share (in exchange for equity), sometimes at the expense of short-term profitability. But when you're bootstrapping, cash flow must drive every major decision. My bosses at the printing company where I cut my teeth wouldn't approve any equipment purchase that couldn't pay for itself in 180 days. It's a strict (some might say extreme) rule, but it certainly kept us grounded in reality. And I've carried that basic philosophy forward. Whether signing a lease or investing in office build-outs, I map out exactly when and how expenses will be recouped. For example, with a five-year lease, I factor in the cost of build-outs, like walls, carpets, and restrooms, so that by the time the lease is up, we've fully recouped those expenses and can enjoy the fruits of higher profitability in the additional five-year renewal period we always negotiate.

These practical considerations aren't glamorous, but they're critical to surviving and thriving in business. Our decision-making for new offices is driven strictly by hard numbers. If an office in Spring Hill requires fifty agents to break even within six months, then that's the target. If we can't achieve that, we don't open the office. It's as simple as that. People often ask why we haven't expanded into certain areas, pointing to smaller brokerages that seem to be doing OK there. What such inquiries completely miss is that those businesses often run on different models that rely on the owner's production to stay afloat.

In business, there's no substitute for a solid cash flow foundation. Everything else—the growth, the impact, and even your peace of mind—stems from having a cash position that allows you to sustain, grow, and ultimately enjoy the work you do.

After reading this chapter, you may be thinking, "There are so many things that can derail my business, from bad partnerships to rising costs, mounting debt, and cash flow. How does any entrepreneur survive?" The answer, ultimately, is simple: by planning carefully, double-checking everything, and practicing good cash flow management.

NINE

THE IMPORTANCE OF SELF-REFLECTION

FTER A WHILE, AS I WAS REHABBING HOUSES, other investors started noticing my success and, knowing I had a license, asked me to help them find and sell properties. Eventually, this brought me to a crossroads. Did I want to continue managing rehab projects, or shift to strictly doing sales and working with investors, where the financial gain could be faster and more profitable?

In late 2003, I chose to pivot into real estate sales, at first joining a local Coldwell Banker franchise. But like most franchises, they took too big a cut of my commissions—35 percent, to be exact. That meant I was getting just 65 cents on every dollar I earned. So I left with a few colleagues and started Hillwood Realtors, a small firm of five partners. Each partner put in about $20,000 to start the company, and we quickly built our roster up to about sixty-five agents, each of whom focused primarily on rehab properties and investors.

Our rapid success caught the attention of a national franchisor who came knocking with a big check in their hand. They wanted us to convert to their brand, so they could expand market share. These deals often involve up-front cash, which is really structured as a loan with a gradual "forgiveness" of that loan over a five-year period, provided the newly franchised brokerage continues to grow and remains affiliated with the brand. My partners—nice people, but mostly salespeople without much strategic business history—were dazzled by the dollar signs and eager to take the deal. I reviewed the paperwork and told them it made sense for them, but not for me. I asked them to buy me out, and I agreed to stay on for a few months to help with the transition. After that (mid-2004), I moved to a different brokerage closer to home and shifted my focus from rehabbing to high-end new construction.

That shift was critical for me. I was burned out from managing fifty-two property transactions a year, each averaging $160,000 in value. It was just me—no assistant, no team—and I realized I couldn't keep up that pace without risking my health and well-being. So, I took a step back and focused on what I did best: navigating the ins and outs of construction and property development. That led me to high-end new builds, where I could leverage my expertise in "sticks and bricks." The shift paid off as a pivotal moment in my real estate career. My volume jumped by $4 million, while my transaction count dropped significantly. In other words, I was doing fewer deals but making more money. That was when I realized how valuable focusing on quality over quantity can be. (If you haven't already discovered that secret for yourself, let me invite you right now to consider it.)

As good as things were, by the end of 2005, I was beginning to chafe under the situation I found myself in. I had paid my broker $64,000 in fees that year on an 80/20 split. That's a fairly traditional model, but the only time I went to the brokerage was to deliver or pick up commission checks. In the meantime, my broker did hardly anything to help my business. So—in the spirit of running at a problem head-on—I went to her and said, "Help me understand this value proposition. I don't use your conference room, your copier, or your office. I don't even see you most days when I stop by the office. Why am I paying you $64,000 a year?"

I thought it was a valid question, especially considering that she had just bought a new Jaguar and renovated the office. After a little back-and-forth, I proposed a new split—90/10—and she refused, offering me a "free" office instead, which I didn't need because I already had one I was paying rent on across town.

That's when I decided it was time to go out on my own. At the time, I was doing about $20 million in sales annually. I reminded her of that, and also of the fact that I held a broker's license, which meant I could legally start my own firm. She brushed it off, but it probably won't surprise you by now to learn that I wouldn't be dissuaded.

Point blank, I asked her, "Has anyone in this organization other than me sold even $10 million in real estate this year? Seven million? Five million?" The answer was no to all three. That conversation sealed the deal for me, and I resolved to leave. That moment was a culmination of so many of the lessons I had learned and have tried to share with you: practicing resilience, demonstrating grit, burning the boats, running at a problem head-on, communicating honestly, and more. In March of 2006, Amanda and I launched Benchmark Realty in the front room of a house in downtown Franklin, with me as the only agent...and I've never looked back.

Starting Benchmark was about more than just leaving a bad deal behind—it was about creating a model that worked not just for me, but for others. I wanted to build something that allowed agents to keep more of what they earned, to have more control over their success, and to thrive in a way that traditional brokerages didn't allow. **And that's what entrepreneurship is all about: creating a system where you and the people around you can win.** That's where the real joy comes from.

ANALYZE WHAT'S WORKING (AND WHAT ISN'T)

Self-reflection is essential to making real progress. Every time I hit a major hurdle in business, I take a step back, try to analyze what's working, and figure out what needs to change. I encourage you to do the same (in life and in business). And when you see the path forward, you can't be afraid to take the bull by the horns and make bold moves. That's exactly what I did when we started Benchmark.

In my second full year in real estate, I closed fifty-six transactions totaling $9 million in sales—all without an assistant. It was just me, grinding it out. That $9 million might sound impressive, but with an average sales price of about $160,000, the volume of transactions required was exhausting. I quickly realized that if I didn't change my approach, I'd burn out fast. This was in late 2004, when Williamson County was booming with high-end new developments, and I saw an opportunity to leverage my deep knowledge of construction.

I took a step back and asked myself, "What do I do best?" Since I had a highly refined understanding of the nuts and bolts of building homes, I refocused on custom home builders, a market segment that was growing rapidly. I began cold-calling builders, asking how I could make myself valuable to them. Then, I moved on to visiting work sites in person so I could meet builders face to face. Initially, I wasn't necessarily trying to pitch them on using me as their agent, but focusing intently on learning as much as I could about what they needed in a real estate agent. It was tough. Many already had long-standing relationships or relied on family members to represent them. Most of the time, I never seemed to catch up with the builder onsite in the developments, but I kept showing up anyway. Eventually I figured out that the typical builder would usually do a tour of all their partially completed houses on Friday afternoon. So, I started showing up about 4:00 on Fridays with a cold six-pack. It's easy to make friends with a builder that way, but most of the time they'd just shoot the breeze, drink a beer, and head off. But I kept pushing, refining my approach, and making the case for why they needed a dedicated sales expert.

Finally, one afternoon, a builder I had spoken with several times phoned me with some angst in his voice, saying he had a problem and wanted my input. He asked to meet at a local restaurant called the Bunganut Pig to discuss it over a beer. His problem was clear: He and his wife, who was acting as his real estate agent, were struggling to separate their work from their personal life. It was affecting both the business and their marriage. I listened to his story. Then he asked the magical question: "She and I just can't work together anymore; what do you think I should do?"

I told him plainly, "I think you should hire me." He did, and he went on to become my largest client and a partner in the brokerage, catapulting Benchmark into a period of rapid growth. The important lesson here: **Never be afraid to advocate for yourself and ask for what you want.**

We found success specializing in what I call "custom spec houses." We'd start with a basic model, find a buyer along the way, and then customize it to meet the buyer's preferences. I was hands-on with every aspect—selecting lots, managing the sales process, doing all the marketing and advertising, writing contracts, and spending most weekends on-site, ready to meet potential buyers. We were selling homes priced around $850,000 at the time, a price point that would easily exceed $1.5 million in today's market. We had high-end homes clustered in popular subdivisions, and the sales were strong. It felt like we had struck gold.

Our brokerage was focused on builders of big-dollar properties. I built Benchmark into a team of thirteen agents while I worked directly with the builders. I was the "rainmaker," pulling in business from about five builders. Everything was going smoothly—until the autumn of 2007. The Great Recession hit the high-end product first, and suddenly, the houses we had listed weren't selling. Literally, it hit so hard and so fast, it was like someone flipped the light switch off but forgot to tell anyone. Simultaneously with this, my largest builder came to me and said, "My houses aren't selling, and I think it's Benchmark's fault, so I'm starting my own real estate brokerage." And as if that wasn't bad enough, it wasn't long before I realized he had enticed seven of my thirteen agents to leave with him before even talking to me.

That was a real gut punch. There I was, kicked to the curb, stomped in the guts, and left with a decision to make: fold my tent and go back to working for someone else, or figure out a new way forward.

It didn't take me long to figure out the answer. Sure, I could've gone back to printing or been hired by any real estate brokerage in town—I probably would've gotten a job in a heartbeat—but that's not who I am. I'm not a quitter. So I dug deep, tapped into the tenacious part of my personality, and decided to knuckle down and figure it out.

At that time, we were operating on an 80/20 split. That model works well enough when the brokerage does a lot for the agents, but this crisis meant we had to do something radically

better, or Benchmark wouldn't survive. So, I started research-
ing what other major markets were doing, especially those that
seemed to be weathering the early stages of the recession better
than we were. I also reached out to every franchisor not already
in Middle Tennessee to look for insights. None of my research
or conversations turned up a bulletproof solution, but we were
staring into the abyss of the recession. I had to come up with
something that made sense.

After exhaustive research, I concluded that a fee-based
model—where agents pay a flat fee per closing instead of a per-
centage of their commission—was much more scalable in light
of the economic conditions. So, I told the few remaining agents
to go home, sell real estate as best they could, and I'd come back
to them with a new plan shortly.

During December 2007 and January 2008, I jettisoned
everything: the office condo, the furniture, and the expenses. I
also rewrote the business plan. We relaunched Benchmark on
February 1, 2008, and began operating under a fee-based model.
Under this new plan, whether agents sold a $100,000 house or
a $10 million mansion, the fee paid to the brokerage would be
the same. Whether the agent charged a 10% commission or a 0%
commission, the fee would be the same. For high producers, this
model offered predictability and jugular control over their broker payout, which is a real estate agent's biggest expense. Because

of the recession, we were literally on the brink of disaster, but you know me. We were going to make it work or die trying, no matter what.

Was it terrifying? Sure. But to be honest, I was too busy to let the fear get hold of me. It's like what soldiers describe when they're in combat—there's fear, but you're so focused on what you need to do to stay alive that you don't have time to panic. That was me. I knew I had to figure it out, so I kept pushing forward. In 2008, we sold maybe $10 million worth of real estate, and I personally sold $6 million of that. For context, just two years prior, in 2006, I had sold nearly $25 million on my own. The drop-off was brutal.

The numbers tell the story: in 2006, I paid taxes on $325,000 in personal income. In 2007, that dropped to $157,000. By 2008, I was paying taxes on just $17,000. That's how fast the recession hit. I was pouring every bit of commission I earned back into the company to keep it afloat. If I hadn't saved a chunk of that 2006 income, I would've been hanging my shingle on someone else's wall for sure (refer back to the earlier discussion regarding cash and debt management, not to mention the discussion about how important it is to have a plan).

By mid-2009, we had about thirty agents, but with the fee-based model, more agents meant less income per head. It took a lot of agents to make up the difference between what we made under the 80/20 model and what we were making after the switch. Those were trying times. Around the second quarter of 2009, I vividly remember having a quiet conversation with God, saying, "Lord, if this doesn't turn soon, I'm going to have to go get a job." And that's when something amazing happened. An agent who was with another brokerage walked into my office and asked if I'd accept her license. Turns out she was sick of the way things were run at her brokerage. I said yes, and within four months, *sixty* more agents followed her.

She was what I call, in a kind and loving way, a "maven"—one of those people to whom others naturally gravitate. I didn't realize it at the time, but hiring her was instrumental in our growth, and I will be forever grateful. Her former franchise owner didn't take it too well, though, and actually accused me of setting up Benchmark just to crucify him. I still shake my head over that. I wasn't out to get him or anyone else; I was just trying to survive, and the rest, as they say, is history.

REFINE, REFINE, REFINE

One of the best perspectives on success I've read recently comes from *Atomic Habits* by James Clear. In the book, Clear references what he calls the "Goldilocks Rule," using comedian Steve Martin as an example. Steve Martin spent ten years learning and honing his craft, another four refining it, and finally, four years in the spotlight as a household name. To most, those last four years looked like overnight success, but in reality, they were the tip of a fourteen-year iceberg of dedication, refinement, and resilience.

People see stories of big-time celebrities who "came out of nowhere," but that is usually only a fraction of the full story. Just like Steve Jobs, Jeff Bezos, and Bill Gates, the truth is those celebrities often had years of relentless hard work and failures before they enjoyed a few shining years of wild success.

This isn't just a showbiz phenomenon. It's the story of every genuine success, yet the myth of the "overnight success" perseveres. Again: Overnight success is the exception, not the rule. But because of that myth, many people give up too soon, killing their own dreams before they have the chance to succeed. Real success in any field, business included, is about getting up every single day, putting on your game face, and grinding when you'd rather be doing anything else. But just as importantly, it's about learning, growing, and adapting to get better at what you do.

I remember this lesson well from my early days in the printing business. After we sold Cantrell Graphics and I got to Lellyett & Rogers, I ended up working alongside a man who was supposedly on the path to become general manager. We were oil and water from the start, and while I liked to think the problem was solely with him, the reality is we simply saw the world differently.

His father-in-law owned a competing print company and had invested a lifetime toward establishing a strong legacy in the industry. But this guy didn't want to do the work, he just wanted the title. His approach to business was more about finding a way to get out of work, hoping he could leave early to hunt or fish, rather than digging in and grinding it out. In other words, he wanted to be the boss without putting in the effort to learn how to run the business.

My time with him taught me that true leaders don't shy away from being out front at all times. Leaders are the first in and the last out, like Colonel Hal Moore, the real-life inspiration for the movie *We Were Soldiers*. Moore, a Vietnam War commander, led with the philosophy, "I'm the first in and the last out." He believed a leader should be there through the toughest times, bringing every wounded and fallen soldier home. It's a mindset that translates to business: **You lead from the front, not from behind.**

Greatness lies in attending to those small, boring details, the minor modifications to a system that ultimately drive success. I often compare the brain to a muscle; the more resistance we push against mentally, the stronger our brains become. And those daily, often monotonous activities create a kind of muscle memory that pulls us through tough times. On days when morale is low—and let's be real, everyone has those days—it's the muscle memory of sticking to your routine, to the daily grind, to processes you've built, that will keep you moving forward.

The most empowering part is that, ultimately, success lies within our control. Sure, there will always be outside factors—economic downturns, divisive elections, natural disasters, and more. But true resilience means focusing on what you can control and using those daily actions to create progress. It's all too easy to let external excuses build up, distracting you from your goals. But in my experience, most people who waste time blaming external circumstances are likely to have the same complaint months down the road when the external circumstance has changed.

Master the mundane. Embrace the boring. Analyze what's working (and what isn't) and make constant minor modifications—over time, they will compound into significant progress. In my experience, when this kind of hard work and dedication becomes second nature, the results will take care of themselves.

CONFRONTING FAILURE

The one guarantee in business is that mistakes and failures are inevitable. The key to long-term success lies not in avoiding these pitfalls, but in quickly and effectively rebounding from them. It's about recovery speed, and I learned early in my career that recovery speed can make or break your relationship with clients.

There were countless times in the printing world when a job would go sideways in the plant, whether it was because the wrong ink was used or a typo slipped through unnoticed. Every printing job runs the risk of an endless gauntlet of human error, so it was routine for someone to mess up, and almost inevitably, the job wouldn't be ready on the day it was supposed to be delivered.

My dad, a seasoned businessman himself, recognized this and gave me advice that has always stuck with me: "Son, never tell someone you have a problem until you have a solution." It wasn't about hiding from the issue, but respecting the customer enough to solve the problem as quickly as possible before delivering the bad news. So instead of just telling a client, "The job won't be ready today," I'd say, "I can have it to you by 3 PM tomorrow, with 2,000 extra copies as a courtesy." That approach took the sting out of the situation. It's much harder to be upset when you hear both the issue and the solution at once. On the other hand, just saying, "I failed," or "I'm sorry," without offering a fix can irreparably damage your credibility. Everyone makes mistakes. It's how you overcome those mistakes that results in success. And you know what? This approach is just as critical on a small scale as it is on a large one.

I took this lesson with me across multiple ventures, including one I haven't told many people about—The Box Company. It all started with my fascination with packaging for communion wafers. (Yeah, I know, I'm weird.) If you've ever seen communion wafers, they come in small, rigid cardboard boxes, typically with a printed wrap advertising the contents. This is a highly specialized business—in fact, there are only about four major communion bread manufacturers in the United States. I got into it because we were printing the box wraps for a guy who owned the machinery to make both the wafers and the boxes. I thought, "Why not leverage that machinery to make boxes for other uses?" With my background in printing, I envisioned rigid business card boxes and letterhead boxes—items that were in high demand at the time. But despite my optimism, that venture failed miserably.

The lesson there wasn't to give up on trying new ideas, but instead to quickly assess what wasn't working and move on. I realized it was better to cut my losses and redirect my energy into new opportunities rather than pour resources into something that didn't have a future.

Not long after The Box Company, I had another idea for something I called "Physician Supply." Back then, doctor's offices relied heavily on paper materials: letterheads, envelopes, prescription pads, and appointment cards. I wanted to create a mail-order catalog for small medical offices that would offer these supplies conveniently. However, I quickly learned that while people want things, they also tend to keep only the freebies and discard the rest. Samples went out, but orders didn't come in the way I had hoped.

Taken together, these failures taught me another valuable lesson: rebounding doesn't mean stubbornly sticking to the same plan, hoping for a different outcome. Instead, it's about recognizing when a concept doesn't work, learning why it failed, and being willing to pivot to the next venture without letting the setback define your capabilities.

There was another lesson buried in there, too: Each failure offered me information, and if I paid attention and figured out what that information was, it would ultimately lead me to greater success in the future. When something doesn't work out, you have to modify, adapt, and move forward, again and again. That doesn't mean you're giving up, nor does it mean you're throwing in the towel. Far from it. Rather, you are refining your understanding of what works and what doesn't and pivoting in a better direction. It's not merely, "I failed," but, "I learned something important that will contribute to future success." This difference in mindset is incredibly important.

Remember, Benchmark was a well-oiled machine in the early days until the mortgage and housing crisis swept in like a tidal wave and wrecked the ship. I was heavily invested in the company: thirteen agents, an employee, an office condo, and a rather elaborately decorated space. And yet, when the recession hit, I had no choice but to make drastic changes and jettison all of it. I slashed every expense I could, consolidated into one small office with just my desk, and got to work figuring out how to survive. I had effectively come back to the starting point of this business, but I was not about to just throw in the towel. I didn't let discouragement determine my direction. Instead, I accepted the hard fact that I had to make changes. That's when I made the radical shift I told you about earlier—the shift to a fee-based model. It was a sustainable path forward. Though we went through some lean years, it kept us afloat. Remember, in that first year after the relaunch, our entire team of five agents sold only $10 million in real estate, with me personally handling about $6 million of that (down from the $25 million I had personally done just two years earlier). We were far from the powerhouse we are today, but it was a start—and, most importantly, it worked.

Fast forward to today, and Benchmark has grown from that scrappy team of five to over 1,750 agents across ten locations in Middle Tennessee and southern Kentucky. We even have our toes into Alabama! This year, we'll likely close in on $5 billion in real estate sales. Yes, that's billion, with a "b," which will in turn result in over $100 million in gross commission income.

Reflecting on that journey, I realize how different the outcome could have been if I'd simply quit back in 2007. The thousands of lives we've touched, the careers we've supported, and the communities we've built wouldn't exist if I'd let that one devastating blow defeat me.

That's the critical lesson: **When failure strikes, it's not about what happened, but about how you react to it.** And sometimes, the most important decision you can make is to simply refuse to give up.

One of the greatest pleasures in my career has been the ability to say, without hesitation, that our work has positively impacted hundreds of thousands of lives. This journey wasn't just about refusing to accept defeat myself; it was about building a culture where defeat was never an option for anyone on our team. Together, we created ripples of impact that spread far beyond the office, out into the community, and to thousands of families.

In the past nineteen years, we've closed over 100,000 transactions. That's more than 100,000 properties that have passed through our hands, each representing a family or an individual finding their home, selling a property, or making a life transition. If you think about that number for a moment—the 100,000 properties we've helped move—the magnitude of that impact quickly becomes very meaningful. Imagine the families behind those transactions: some are one- or two-person households, others four or more. Add in our agents, their families, our employees and their families, and we're well beyond a quarter of a million people—possibly as high as half a million people—whose lives have been touched by our work.

And the impact doesn't end there. Over the years, our success has enabled us to give back through philanthropic and multiple ministry efforts that have further expanded this ripple effect. It's impossible to calculate the full impact, but it's likely to be many multiples beyond just the direct connections—perhaps even five or six times the original count.

That's the true cost of giving up: those opportunities would never have come to fruition, those families would never have been helped, and that larger community impact would never have been realized if we had thrown in the towel in 2007 or 2008. And that's why refusing to quit matters so much.

I credit much of my resilience to the lessons my dad instilled in me, including his advice to "always have the solution." It wasn't just a guideline for work; it became a principle for life. And I couldn't have done any of this without my wife, Amanda. She's been a steadfast supporter, always encouraging me with her simple message: "Do what you need to do." She's my rock, my favorite person, and my greatest advocate. Having that kind of support system is priceless. It's not in any business notes or financial reports, but it's a key ingredient for success. If things aren't working at home, it's nearly impossible to make anything work in business. I know this all too well from my own years feeling stuck in printing for nearly two decades without the right support.

Building this company, creating these ripples, and impacting lives are the results of dedication, refinement, family support, and a refusal to accept defeat. That's the real legacy we're building—one that reaches beyond us into families, communities, and future generations.

DON'T BLAME OTHERS FOR YOUR STRUGGLES

How you respond to challenges and setbacks is incredibly important, but just as important is *who you choose to blame*. When the business is falling apart, some leaders immediately start looking for someone to blame. The owner of that franchise, for example, had apparently created a toxic culture that pushed agents away, and instead of looking inward to fix it, he blamed me when his agents jumped ship.

Most of the time, the struggles in your business are a reflection of what's happening inside. Your success or failure is on you—the person in the mirror. There will always be external factors, but if you focus on those too much, you're just making excuses. Instead, **focus on what you can learn from the struggle and how you can apply those lessons to do better.**

It wasn't until 2011 that I hired my first principal broker and split my roles of running operations and managing agents. I accepted that if I didn't make that move, I would be holding the company back. I was doing too much—acting as the principal broker, managing all the operations, and selling at the same time. By 2012, I took another big step and stopped selling entirely so I could focus on working *on* the business instead of *in* it. That's when Benchmark really started to take off.

Every entrepreneur will face moments when they're tempted to give in to the "woe is me" mindset. I've had my share of those moments too. But when that voice creeps in, you have to tell yourself, "Stop it. Get over yourself. This isn't who you are." Everyone struggles, but what defines you is whether you let those struggles stop you or refine you. Do you let them push you forward or turn you into a bitter person with a scarcity mentality? I could've kept trying to do everything and blamed any lack of growth on everyone and everything else. Instead, I took a good hard look in the mirror and decided to make changes that would benefit the business, our agents, and myself.

A longtime colleague of mine runs a major franchisor on the West Coast. He has over 6,000 agents and grew up in the business, so we often find ourselves discussing the industry and what's working for us. He clearly demonstrates that if you drop all the complaining and petty competition and stop blaming other people for your struggles, there's actually a lot of camaraderie to be found in this industry. We face similar struggles, have walked similar paths, and when you take the time to build real relationships, they can help support you through those tough moments. Sometimes, though, you just have to tell yourself to pull your head out of your ass and get to work. Don't look for someone else to blame. Analyze what's not working, make adjustments, refine your processes, and keep the wheels turning. Modify, adapt, move forward. Repeat.

WHAT DID YOU LEARN TODAY?

Remember: Experience alone isn't enough for success. If we don't take the time to reflect on it, to record it, and to really think about what it means for the future, then that experience is essentially wasted. This is particularly true in the real estate industry. Every day, thousands of agents wake up like it's a brand new day in real estate, with little continuity from yesterday's lessons. It blows my mind. That approach, in my view, is a huge mistake. If you're approaching the real estate business like it's a fresh start every day (instead of building on your past), you're setting yourself up for an inconsistent income stream and, likely, burnout.

To avoid that, I try to ask myself one simple question each night: *What did I learn today, and how can this help me tomorrow?* I have a little black notebook I carry around just for this purpose. Sometimes, I write something down without fully understanding its value in the moment, only to realize its significance months or even years later. These notes might capture a lesson, an insight, or even just a small detail from an encounter that for some reason seemed important at the time. And sure enough, over time, those insights accumulate and become invaluable touchpoints that can shape future decisions.

One of the notes I remember jotting down is, "We're the sum total of our experiences." The more we actively engage with and remember our lessons, the better equipped we are to navigate what's next—and to help others do the same. It's a discipline I've tried to maintain consistently, because **our past is a resource we can revisit and apply**. And you know what? That idea alone is worth committing to memory.

TEN

ALWAYS LEARNING, ALWAYS IMPROVING

ROCESSES ARE THE LIFEBLOOD OF ANY SUCCESS-ful business. A strong process can make everything smoother, more reliable, and ultimately, more automatable. Having the right processes in place will allow you to consistently achieve the highest standards no matter how your business, industry, and/or market shift or scale.

If you want an impressive example of this in action, look no further than Chick-fil-A. If you've ever been there—or if, like me, you're willing to spend a little time in their parking lot just observing—you'll see a logistics masterpiece in motion. People are obsessed with Chick-fil-A's efficiency, and for a good reason. They've taken the concept of process control to a level that's almost an art form. They're constantly fine-tuning *everything*. From the layout of their parking lot to the number of cash registers, they continually adapt to maximize their drive-through capacity because, after deeply studying their own operations, they know that's where most of their business comes from.

Recently, I noticed the store near my office cut down on the number of cashiers inside but added more drive-through stations. They also added more employees out in the drive-through lanes taking orders on iPads. You no longer have to stop at a menu board and talk to a microphone during peak hours. Instead, you speak directly with someone face-to-face. And have you ever noticed how much faster a debit card approves on their system versus the competition's? Theirs is instantaneous, while others take as much as 30 seconds. Cumulatively, this results in exponentially higher daily throughput for them. Small adjustments that make the whole experience more seamless, and for me, watching this machine in action is like watching a well-rehearsed dance. Each movement, each step, is a perfectly choreographed process.

The power of this model is simple: incremental changes lead to exponential advantages. A minor tweak here and a small adjustment there add up to massive improvements over time. The Chick-fil-A system is so well-designed, in fact, that it functions smoothly even with young, minimally trained workers at the helm. Because the processes are so robust, there's little room for failure.

This example emphatically illustrates the fact that when you put your focus on processes, you become less dependent on any single individual or personality. Please don't misunderstand me: Of course people make a business come alive. But when people inevitably move on, whether they marry, relocate, or simply seek new experiences, a solid process structure ensures that your business doesn't stumble and the service delivery to your consumer remains consistent. Think of it in terms of the human body's skeletal system, where people are the muscles and the processes are the bones that keep everything standing.

In industries like hospitality, you'll often hear excuses about not having enough people as a reason for poor service. How many times have you walked into a restaurant with half their tables empty only to be told there's a wait because they don't have enough staff to serve? The truth is, that's not really a staffing problem, it's a process problem. When a business relies too heavily on "good people" rather than good processes, they're often unable to function effectively when staff numbers dip. A well-designed process removes that barrier.

Ultimately, this particular lesson is simple yet powerful: **Your business is both the people and the processes.** The people provide the energy and personality, but it's the processes that provide structure, reliability, and the ability to scale or adapt, regardless of who's filling each role. And here's the real key: There are always improvements to be made. People can learn and grow, and processes can be refined. That's why it is so important to be a constant learner.

FOCUS ON LEARNING—CONTINUALLY

Business leaders often reach a certain level and think, "I've made it. I know enough to keep this going." That's a limiting mindset to have. What they don't realize is that the landscape is always changing. The ground beneath them is constantly moving, and if they settle into complacency, they'll eventually lose their footing. The day you stop learning is the day you start declining.

Every leader should be reading voraciously, absorbing everything they can each day. To stay sharp, you have to constantly seek knowledge. That's the foundation of sustainable success. Staying curious and learning daily has a hidden benefit beyond just expanding knowledge—it keeps you grounded. The moment you start thinking you're the smartest person in the room, you're in dangerous territory. That kind of hubris has led many companies to their downfall.

Jim Collins talks about this in his book *How the Mighty Fall*. He studied twenty-five companies and examined how they went from success to failure, often identifying a key moment of arrogance as the starting point of their decline. Collins breaks it down into five distinct stages, with stage one being a belief in your own hype—believing you're the best, untouchable, hitting every note perfectly, and therefore have no reason to keep improving.

Don't get me wrong; celebrating wins is important. But the moment an organization or a leader believes they're unassailable is when the real trouble begins. I've taken that lesson to heart throughout my career, but the true value of it has only become clear with time. After four decades of experience, I know that success is built on continuously refining and honing what works.

This idea is evident in science, too. Every scientific breakthrough stands on the shoulders of previous work. It's the same in business. If you aren't constantly learning, you won't understand the foundation others have laid, and you'll miss the chance to build on it. Without that foundation, you can end up blinded by your own arrogance, believing you've got it all figured out. That kind of attitude prevents you from seeing the facts and opportunities right in front of you.

Learning every day keeps you sharp and open and enables you to stay in sync with the world around you. Put bluntly, **no matter what level of success you achieve, there's always more to learn.**

How do you keep learning? By reading widely, by cross-referencing ideas, and by constantly exposing yourself to multiple perspectives and viewpoints. I still attend at least five conferences a year. Not only do I learn from speakers in my industry, but I get to sit down with other pros in "Lobby Con," as we call it—the real deal-making in the convention center lobbies. We're there sharing challenges, solutions, and ideas. Those exchanges are invaluable.

That said, I'm not one for idle chit-chat. If I'm at a networking event, I'm there to dig deep. People I talk to probably walk away exhausted, thinking, "Man, I was just trying to have a drink." But the knowledge you can gain in those moments is worth more than any casual cocktail hour. Every interaction is a chance to challenge my thinking, and that's how I like it.

We talked about it earlier, but one of the biggest barriers to growth is fear. Fear kills more dreams than any obstacle on earth. Success is a mental game, played 100 percent between the ears. And fear is often driven by the unknown, by not keeping up with what's happening around you. I'm not talking about keeping up with the news cycle, either; I'm talking about digging deep into your profession. If you aren't keeping yourself educated, you'll get blindsided as things inevitably change. The universe is in a constant state of flux—physically, spiritually, and every other possible way. You either embrace that and keep learning, or you let fear paralyze you and remain stranded as things evolve.

That's why my home office is a library filled with an extraordinary number of books. Visitors are often awed when they see them and ask if I've read them all. My answer is always the same: "Yes, and many more. These are just the ones I decided to keep so I can refer back to them." These books are more than pages on a shelf. They are tools I've returned to time and time again, marked with highlighters and tabs, their wisdom woven into the fabric of my decisions. I also listen to 60 to 70 Audible books a year, and many of them become part of my regular rotation. If a book resonates deeply, I'll often buy a hard copy and read it again (usually with a highlighter in hand). There's something powerful about combining auditory and visual learning—it solidifies the message in a way that feels permanent.

Personally, I start my day at the office with about 45 minutes of learning, whether it's by reading books, trade journals, industry news, relevant articles, or watching a recorded podcast. This daily habit of learning and sharpening my skills keeps me agile and informed, and it's something I believe every leader should embrace. It's like the proverb "iron sharpens iron." I also try to spend about thirty minutes each morning at home dedicated to personal growth and reflection through contemplation, prayer, and Bible study. This is a grounding ritual for me—a time to align my thoughts and priorities before diving into the day.

In the evenings, my exercise routine doubles as another opportunity to learn. I'm a big walker, and what started as an hour-and-a-half routine has now stretched to two hours many days. Whether it's walking outdoors or working out, I'm always listening to something educational. The key is consistency. You can't afford to let yourself stagnate, especially in a world that's constantly evolving.

YOU CAN BE THE LION

Continuous learning is a necessity for leadership. In the real estate brokerage world, I've noticed a troubling pattern. Many brokers and owners are exceptional technicians who have sold their way to the top, but they lack the business acumen needed to manage the complexities of running a brokerage. This isn't unique to real estate. It's a symptom of what I call *entrepreneurial delusion.* People fantasize about having the rewards of leadership without embracing the responsibilities. They love the idea of being the lion but shy away from the hard work it takes to do lion things.

But here's the thing: *You can be the lion.* It just takes commitment and the humility to continually educate yourself. The smartest leaders in the room are the ones who know they're *not* the smartest person in the room. That realization means they're willing to listen, adapt, and apply what they learn to their own struggles and challenges.

Perhaps you're familiar with Murphy's Law, which is often misunderstood as "anything that can go wrong will go wrong." The original phrasing of Murphy's Law, which was coined by aerospace engineer Edward Murphy Jr., is actually far more profound: *"If there are two or more ways to do something, and one of those ways can result in catastrophe, someone will do it that way."* Murphy's insight isn't about catastrophizing—it's about preparing. It speaks to the importance of analyzing patterns and learning from the mistakes of others to avoid stepping on the same landmines. And that's why, if this book helps even one person avoid some of the mistakes I've made, I will consider it a success.

The value of knowledge, however, lies not in its accumulation but in its application. This principle is embodied in another saying, Wilson's Law, which states, *"Knowledge and intelligence are the key drivers of wealth accumulation, and the application of knowledge leads to success."* Operative word here: *application.* Simply put, it's not enough to read a book or attend a seminar. Success comes from taking what you've learned and putting it into action.

This is an important concept, so let me put it another way: **The pursuit of continuous learning is not about perfection but about progress.** If you can take just one lesson, apply it, and make a difference in your life or your business, then the effort has been worth it. As I see it, success isn't about avoiding mistakes altogether but about learning from them and using that knowledge to help others along the way.

So, yes, I listen to a staggering number of audiobooks—well over 300 hours in 2024 alone—but simply consuming content isn't enough. For knowledge to be transformative, it has to be refined and tailored to your style and goals. It's like sanding down a rough piece of wood until it fits perfectly into the structure you're building. This is part of what I wrote about earlier with learning to "get comfortable with the boring." The consistent effort of learning and applying may not be glamorous, but it's critical to achieving meaningful outcomes. Reading one book won't make you rich, but reading dozens, applying what you've learned, and iterating on those lessons *will*. It's not about speed or quantity, but depth and follow-through.

I'm acutely aware that some people argue that attention spans are shrinking and traditional learning methods are outdated. They point to social media and YouTube as the go-to tools for quick insights. They have a point, but while these platforms have value, they are *supplements* to the kind of study I'm talking about, *not substitutes*. Learning must be deliberate and integrated into your long-term strategy. The method doesn't matter as much as maintaining a solid commitment to learn, adapt, and grow.

LEARN FROM THE PAST

Along with study, I also spend a significant amount of time look-ing inward and reflecting on my own patterns and responses. Often, I'll bounce my thoughts off my wife because she can serve as a mirror, helping me see areas I might otherwise over-look. I trust her to hold up that mirror and offer insights that help me stay grounded and grow, which is something I think every leader needs.

I believe it's important to reflect on your past often and con-sider the lessons you've learned along the way. As Aristotle put it, *"A society that loses its grip on the past is in danger, for it produces men who know nothing about the present and who are not aware that life has been and could be different from what it is."*

Reflecting on the past is essential for growth and improve-ment, both personally and professionally. The sum total of our experiences provides the foundation for every decision we make and allows us to navigate future challenges with wisdom. To paraphrase the book of Ecclesiastes in the Bible, "There is noth-ing new under the sun." The mistakes we're trying to avoid have been made before. It's up to us to recognize those patterns, learn from them, and step forward with intention.

There's a story that Earl Nightingale used to tell, and it's one that's stuck with me over the years. It goes something like this:

A father comes home from work, changes out of his suit, and settles in to read the evening newspaper. His child, eager for attention, is playing nearby, asking questions, pulling him out of his focus. The father, hoping to find a way to keep the child occupied, comes up with a quick game. He takes a full-page ad from the newspaper that has an image of the earth, tears it into fifteen pieces, and hands it to the child.

"Here, put this back together for me," he says, thinking it will keep the child busy for a while.

But to his surprise, the child returns just a few minutes later with the pieces perfectly arranged. The father, astonished, asks, "How did you do that so quickly?"

The child flips the page around, revealing a picture of a man on the reverse side. "I just put the man together," the child says, "and the world came together."

That story holds a profound truth. When we put ourselves together—when we work on aligning our own values, principles, and purpose—everything around us falls into place. As leaders, it's our responsibility to work on ourselves first. Only then can we bring order, clarity, and focus to the larger world around us.

The idea that *"when the man is together, his whole world is together"* is a message I've carried with me over the years. Especially now, in a time when polarization seems to divide us along every possible line, it's refreshing to focus on the individual. When we're whole and grounded within ourselves, we're less rattled by external differences and less likely to let disagreements prevent us from working together. No matter how chaotic things appear, bringing yourself into alignment makes it easier to face the world with clarity and resolve.

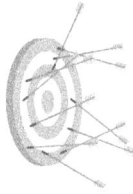

ELEVEN

THE ART OF PATIENCE

N EXT UP, ALLOW ME TO ENCOURAGE YOU TO develop patience. Take the time to make decisions carefully and thoughtfully. In today's fast-paced world, the urge to act immediately can be overwhelming, especially for Type A personalities who thrive on urgency. But, unless you are a demolition expert, few decisions actually require great haste.

For example, when evaluating a major equipment purchase for a printing plant, the shiny new machinery might look irresistible, but a studied approach is important. Same thing with evaluating a piece of technology for a real estate brokerage. First, run the numbers. What's the return on investment? How much will it increase sales? How long will it take to recoup the cost in profits? Next, sleep on it, then recheck your calculations to ensure the decision aligns with your long-term goals. Then, having given it careful and deliberate consideration, *act*. This process will ensure that your decision is not just reactive but strategically sound.

This principle applies to broader business operations as well. Many entrepreneurs fall into the trap of constantly "putting out fires." While some fires are inevitable, a business constantly in crisis is either growing too quickly or lacks proper systems. In some cases, entrepreneurs themselves create problems to solve, driven by a subconscious desire to appear to be the hero. This "entrepreneurial Munchausen syndrome" stems from ego, and it's unsustainable.

A mature approach to leadership involves stepping back and empowering others to find solutions. Instead of solving every problem yourself, ask your team for their recommendations and give them space to implement solutions. As General George S. Patton once said, "Never tell people how to do things. Tell them what to do and they will surprise you with their ingenuity." This not only reduces your stress but also fosters a culture of autonomy and growth.

Remember that **your business isn't about you.** It's about the systems and people that make it work. A business that's overly reliant on one person, even its founder, is a business destined to stall. The goal isn't to build a monument to yourself but to create something lasting and scalable.

Lifelong learning and patient, deliberate decision-making are two sides of the same coin. Together, they form the foundation for sustainable growth and success. By prioritizing knowledge and applying it strategically, you can build a business that thrives. And by taking the time to make thoughtful, informed decisions, you ensure that your business is equipped to grow beyond your individual contributions.

At the same time, you don't want to be *too* patient. *Analysis paralysis*, the trap of overthinking, can stall even the most capable leader. Effective decision-making requires a balance between gathering the facts, studying the situation, and acting decisively when the time comes. There's a temptation to keep searching for more information and wait for the perfect moment. But the reality is, sometimes you have to leap with the knowledge you have.

You must walk the fine line between urgency and preparation, neither rushing nor procrastinating but knowing when it's time to move forward. This kind of balanced decisiveness isn't easy. In fact, an effective leader must sometimes be the "bad guy." You have to make hard decisions and enforce accountability to make sure your organization keeps moving toward its goals. If you're determined to be liked, you will struggle as a leader. As

I often say, "If you're looking for a friend, get a dog. Leadership is about doing what's best for the organization, not winning a popularity contest."

That doesn't mean you should ever be cruel or dismissive. A good leader is always respectful. At the same time, you can't shy away from the tough calls. Entrepreneurs who hesitate often see their businesses stagnate or falter. Growth requires grit, and sometimes, being the bad guy is simply part of the job. Perseverance through the hard moments, the willingness to face the gaping chasm in front of you and press forward, is what separates successful leaders from those who falter.

ACCEPTING DIVERSE VOICES

So often, I hear people whining about what can't be done or complaining about someone else's approach. But criticism without action is just noise. I can't stand it when people point out problems but don't offer solutions. That's not constructive—that's just complaining. Solutions come from action, from putting your head down and tackling the problem, even if it's going to hurt.

That's why I surround myself with people who don't just criticize for the sake of criticizing, but who bring well-thought-out alternatives to the table. If someone doesn't like my approach, that is perfectly fine, but I expect them to present a better option.

I would say this directly to anyone on my team. If someone isn't offering creative input, I'm not interested in hearing them out. In fact, I have this message taped to the bottom of my computer monitor: "Do not trust ideas divorced from execution."

To be clear, I am not dismissive of criticism. Far from it. *Constructive* feedback is incredibly valuable, but it has to include a *solution*. Any conversation or process has positive and negative inputs; when paired with an alternative approach, constructive feedback is always welcome. It's criticism without solutions that drains energy and muddies the waters.

There's another aspect of constructive feedback that is important to understand. Each of us is the sum total of our personal experiences, so we shouldn't expect others to think or act exactly as we would. For leaders, it's important to accept that diversity of thought is a strength. When we expect others to mirror our own decision-making style, we constrict, and will eventually choke off the creative potential within our teams.

I'll admit, this one is tough for me personally. I tend to think, "Why don't they see it *this* way?" or "Why aren't they handling it how I would?" And this tendency can create friction. My wife is quick to remind me of this when we're deep in conversation. She'll say, "Honey, not everyone thinks like you," while probably muttering under her breath, "And thank God for that." She's absolutely right, of course. I can't expect everyone to approach problems with my perspective, and if I keep pushing my way of doing things on others, I will end up frustrated—and so will they.

In leadership, the dividing line between doing your best and letting go is different in every relationship and organizational structure. You can lay out the processes, communicate with clarity, and guide with purpose, but you can't force others to respond exactly as you would. At some point, you have to trust them to do their best, and if they don't meet expectations, that's a separate issue to address.

Look, I get it: Letting go isn't easy. Even talking about it makes me a bit queasy. But I've come to see that releasing control and trusting others is part of growth—both theirs and mine. As leaders, when we stop expecting ourselves from others, we create space for diverse ideas and approaches. That's when our teams can truly thrive. And the irony is when we do this, we're not only more effective but also more at peace within ourselves.

It took me years to accept that I can't expect everyone to operate at my level. I want people to rise to that standard, to match the same level of knowledge and expertise I've built over years of grinding it out. But experience has taught me that this expectation is one of my biggest challenges as a leader. I can get frustrated when others don't "get it" in the same way I do.

Even my company president has pointed out that I need to dial it back, reminding me, "They're not going to get what you're saying if you're talking *at* them rather than *to* them." And he's right. It's a delicate balance because if I push too hard, people stop listening. And if you lose people's attention, you lose their engagement.

The hard truth is that growth as an entrepreneur means confronting those areas where resistance flares up. Leaning into those tough spots is where the real progress happens. And if you happen to work with family or a partner, there's a whole other layer to that challenge. Family dynamics can be far more complex than any business relationship. My son works in operations at Benchmark, while my daughter handles real estate sales, and we've structured our roles very carefully. My son reports to someone else—he doesn't report directly to me. And we have rules about not discussing business outside of work, except in broad, positive terms. If we need to hash something out, we do it in the office, but when we step outside, we're a unified front.

Eisenhower had a saying among his generals: "When we're developing a plan behind closed doors, we can argue it out as much as we want. But when we walk out that door, we're all pushing in the same direction." That principle is vital, especially when family is involved. I've learned from experience how important it is to set clear boundaries so business stress doesn't bleed into personal relationships.

THE TOUGHNESS TO KEEP GOING

Putting all of these lessons into practice requires an extraordinary amount of toughness. Let me give you an example of what I mean. On October 14, 1912, while campaigning in Milwaukee for a third presidential term as a candidate of the Progressive Party (also called the "Bull Moose Party"), Teddy Roosevelt was shot in the chest by a delusional man named John Schrank. The bullet was slowed by his thick coat, the eyeglass case in his pocket, and a folded copy of his upcoming speech.

Famously, despite being shot, he insisted on giving his ninety-minute speech. He began the speech by trumpeting, "It takes more than [a bullet] to kill a Bull Moose!" He showed the attendees the bullet hole in his coat, then he held the bloody pages of his speech aloft. After the speech, he was taken to the hospital, but doctors decided it was too risky to try to remove the bullet. So he carried that bullet in his body, lodged in his chest, until the day he died.

I'm not saying we should all walk around with bullets inside us, but this story exemplifies the toughness and perseverance required to keep going, no matter the obstacles. In entrepreneurship, "the cowards never start, and the weak die along the way." That Kit Carson quote always struck me as a fitting descriptor for the journey. You have to walk through challenges, not just celebrate breakthroughs.

At the same time, success isn't worth much if it doesn't help others along the way. Progress only happens when you keep moving forward, no matter how small the steps. Never quit, because an ordinary life leads to ordinary stories.

GROWTH ISN'T AN ACCIDENT

Growth doesn't just happen—it requires intentional design. Boutique businesses are fine, but if you want scale, that takes intentionality, strategy, and structure. Growth needs to be baked into the design from the start, not something that happens by accident. Success in building a scalable business means having a clear intention and plan from day one.

It isn't enough to just have passion or a good product. You need to be intentional from the outset about planning and setting up systems to handle growth. Too many businesses fail because they don't solve a significant problem for enough people. That's why, from the outset, every business plan must address two questions: *What problem are you solving?* and *How are you going to remove the roadblocks for your customers?* If you're not solving a big enough issue or addressing a real pain point, the business won't have a solid foundation to scale.

Analyze your competitors. Look at the challenges they're bulldozing through and ask yourself if there's a way to smooth out those rough edges in your own business. In real estate, for example, there's an immense amount of friction in the sales process. From listing a house to finalizing the sale, there are countless steps that must be followed. Many of those steps are set in stone, but if you focus on removing as much friction as possible within each one, you'll give your customers a smoother experience. And when customers encounter less friction, you can scale much faster. We've done this in our firm by making incremental improvements that, over time, have added up to a significant competitive advantage.

I didn't always have this clarity. Reflecting on my own experiences, I've had both wins and losses. The losses were often due to insufficient research. I didn't study the market well enough before diving in, or I made poor partnership decisions. Early on, I entered some businesses out of passion without fully understanding whether there was a sustainable demand for what I was offering.

A lot of entrepreneurs fall into this trap. They start businesses because they're passionate about something and believe everyone else will be too, or because they believe it will give them "freedom." But if your product or service doesn't address a *real* need for a large enough customer base, it'll likely remain a boutique business, not a scalable enterprise. It's like putting a ladder against the wrong wall. You can climb as hard and fast as you want, but if the ladder is in the wrong place, you will end up nowhere meaningful. I learned this lesson the hard way after many years at Lellyett & Rogers, where I realized too late that I'd been climbing a corporate ladder that led to a dead end. So, before investing time and resources, always ask, *"What problem does my business solve, and how many people need that solution?"*

Amazon is a great example of what I mean. Their success isn't based on a single product because their real product is convenience. They've solved a universal pain point—time scarcity—by delivering anything you need, right to your door, often within hours. They didn't just fall in love with an idea. They targeted a widespread problem and designed a streamlined solution around it. That's the difference between a business that scales and one that stalls.

When I ventured into the market for business card boxes, I assumed there was a need, but I hadn't identified any real pain point. Similarly, with physician supplies, I hadn't offered a strong enough solution to an urgent enough problem. In both cases, the market wasn't big enough, and I didn't have a unique solution. The ventures didn't take off because there wasn't enough customer pain to solve. If I'd paused and asked myself these core questions from the beginning, I might have saved myself the struggle—and avoided adding those two ventures to my "loss" column.

So, here's the fundamental first question for any entrepreneur: **What is the pain point my business will solve, and how big is the demand for that solution?**

Without answering that question, all the passion and processes in the world won't build a business that lasts. So take the time (in other words, be patient enough) to figure this out *before* you charge ahead. Remember, perseverance, preparation, and planning are all close relatives of patience.

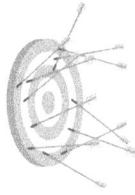

TWELVE

ADAPTING TO MEET NEW CHALLENGES

I F BENCHMARK'S JOURNEY FROM ITS EARLY DAYS TO its peak and eventual sale reveals anything about entrepreneurship, it's this: Being an entrepreneur is a rollercoaster of highs and lows. But through it all, the thrill of building something meaningful, adapting to new challenges, and helping others achieve their goals have made it all worthwhile. For me, the entire experience has reinforced the fact that success in business isn't just about having great ideas—it's about having the grit to execute them effectively, no matter what obstacles stand in the way.

The evolution of Benchmark was driven by necessity and fueled by a relentless commitment to rethink traditional real estate models. When the financial crisis hit in 2007, we didn't just focus on surviving the mortgage crisis; we adapted in order to thrive in its aftermath. We built a resilient, scalable business that could withstand market fluctuations, attract top talent, and deliver consistent value. The early years were a grind, but they set the foundation for what would become a lasting legacy in the real estate industry.

Pivoting and coming up with a new plan was crucial to our success. Interestingly, though, when I discuss Benchmark's growth and success, I often get asked if we strictly followed our original business plan. The answer is: not exactly. The true purpose of a business plan isn't to give you a rigid roadmap but rather to plant a clear direction in your mind. Once you have that vision imprinted, it guides your decision-making almost subconsciously. I'm a tactile learner. I write things down, file the paper away, and still retain the core ideas. That's how the business plan worked for me. Over the years, I've only revisited it twice. And yet, both times I've looked at it, I was amazed to see we were tracking almost exactly to the timeline and financial projections I originally made.

This surprised me and yet, in a way, it didn't. It's like setting goals: If you don't write them down, they're just wishes. Writing down your vision implants it into your subconscious and creates an invisible map that steers everything you do. That is why I tell people, when they ask if I ever imagined Benchmark becoming what it is today, that it's like raising a child. When a baby is born, if someone asks you how big and strong you hope they'll become, your answer is probably, "As big and strong as they possibly can be." That's how I approached Benchmark. I nurtured it so it could grow as much as it was capable of growing...and just like a parent with their child, I couldn't be prouder of the success the company has achieved.

PAYING ATTENTION AND BEING PRESENT

A big part of this success came because I committed to staying alert and paying attention. I've always seen myself as a student of the industry, paying close attention to details others might overlook. I have an unusual knack for spotting out-of-place things in a room or a business process that others walk right past. It might be a birth defect or a quirk in my wiring, but it serves me well. Whether it's noticing inefficiencies in a process or picking up on subtle business signals, I often find myself pointing out things that make people stop and think, "How did I miss that?"

This attentiveness extends beyond processes to people and opportunities. I pay attention to what's being said, triangulate the information, and then act. More than once, I've approached a struggling business owner with an offer to help, only to hear them say, "Thank God you showed up. How did you know?" It's simple: I pay attention. It's a skill I've learned to harness effectively.

Resilience has been another key factor. When I first started pursuing custom home builders, I didn't rely only on emails or online outreach. Instead, I put in the legwork—literally. I would drive out to subdivisions under construction every day, asking around, making friends with subcontractors, and getting introductions to the builders. It was old-fashioned shoe-leather effort, and it worked. In today's digital age, it's almost unheard of, but back then, it was the best way to build relationships.

There's an old saying: "Get up, dress up, show up." **We've become so accustomed to hiding behind screens and keyboards that the value of physical presence is often overlooked.** People crave real connections, and I've built my career on being there in person. Just recently, a prospective recruit reached out to me—an agent who had been following me on social media for over a year. He decided it was time to make a change and wanted to join Benchmark with his wife and daughter, who are also in the business. I didn't leave it to chance. Even though we had been connected on social media for a long time, I set up a physical meeting with our principal broker and made sure to be there in person.

We're real people, building real relationships, and that's why clients and agents choose Benchmark. It's not just the business model or the plan—it's the human element, the face-to-face connections that create trust and make all the difference.

As the world becomes more digitally focused, I find myself constantly telling people, "Just pick up the phone and talk to them." Direct communication is a fundamental principle that's often overlooked in today's business environment. Set yourself apart from the crowd and figure out where you can operate face-to-face, too.

TIPS FOR EXPANDING YOUR BUSINESS

When we started expanding Benchmark beyond its original location, this mindset of direct communication and careful planning guided us through each step of the process. That said, I'll admit that the first expansion is always the hardest. It's nerve-wracking because you're stepping into the unknown. But once you take the leap and realize, "We did it, and nobody died," it becomes easier to repeat.

Our first major expansion was the Midtown office in Nashville. It came about almost by accident. One day, a frustrated colleague called me up and suggested meeting for lunch. He didn't initially mention opening an office, but as we talked, he asked if I'd ever considered starting a Midtown location. I told him I'd go wherever the opportunity was. For me, the criteria for opening a new office is simple: Can we build enough of a market presence to be profitable within 90 to 120 days? If the math works, we move forward. If it doesn't, we don't force it. In this case, the math did work, and eleven years later it's still one of our most successful offices.

In business, it's important to stick to the basic criteria and avoid the trap of chasing shiny objects. I see it all the time: business owners get distracted by the allure of a new location or project and convince themselves it's a must-have. But if the numbers don't add up, no amount of wishful thinking will make it work. **If you spend more than you take in, you won't last long.**

It took me a while to refine the process of figuring out what we could and couldn't do and understanding our financial overhead. Once I had that dialed in, expansion became about identifying opportunities that fit within our proven model.

Nashville is a large market with over 15,000 licensed agents, so opening additional offices in the city was a straightforward decision. However, when we considered more rural areas like Murfreesboro, Clarksville, or Bowling Green, it was a different story. Out in these rural areas, the ratios are different, and the margins can be much tighter. We needed a way to test the waters without overcommitting resources.

That's when we introduced a new concept: *the satellite workspace*. Think of it as a WeWork setup. It's an unstaffed, no-signage, keycard-access facility where agents can meet clients; use copiers, printers, and workstations; and rent offices if needed. It's not an official Benchmark office—there's no full-time staff, which saves us a significant amount in overhead costs. Typically, hiring an admin and a principal broker would cost around $200,000 a year. By using the satellite workspace model, we can provide a place for agents to work without incurring those expenses. Agents appreciate having a physical space close by, and it gives us a foothold in the market without the full commitment of opening a staffed office.

Once we see traction at a satellite location, we can pivot quickly. If enough agents start working there and building momentum, we can put up signage, hire staff, and convert it into a fully operational office. This approach allows us to ease into new markets without deviating from our core business model. It's a strategy based on intuition, driven by math, and grounded in the realities of scaling a business effectively.

In every new market, we expect some resistance (remember the attacks of the naysayers). The local brokers will often talk behind our backs, calling us carpetbaggers or worse. They tell their agents not to pay attention to us, spreading rumors, and trying to undermine our efforts. It's part of the game—an ugly part, but a part nevertheless. I don't let it bother me, and I coach my people to ignore it, too. Instead, we stay focused on what matters: *Delivering value, being present, and building real relationships.*

Our methodical approach—*test, learn, adapt*—has proven itself time and time again. It's not about rushing in or making flashy moves; it's about making smart, calculated decisions based on data and real-world feedback. By easing into new territories with satellite workspaces, we minimize risk while positioning ourselves to capitalize on opportunities as they arise. This strategy has been instrumental in Benchmark's growth, and it has allowed us to expand steadily without sacrificing stability or getting caught up in the frenzy of rapid, unsustainable growth.

PEOPLE YOU CAN TRUST

In Tennessee, real estate rules require each office to have a principal broker, and it's impossible for me to directly manage every location. So, how do I ensure that the people I trust with these roles truly understand our vision and uphold our values?

In the early days, I wore all the hats: principal broker, CEO, admin, even janitor (and I'll level with you: I still take the trash out sometimes). As we grew, I had to learn how to delegate and trust others with these responsibilities. My first step was hiring a principal broker and an admin person for our Franklin office. This was the first time I divided my job and handed a portion of it over to someone else. It was a big step, and it required a lot of hand-holding in the beginning. I had to walk alongside these new leaders to ensure they fully grasped our approach. I can't tell you how many times I said to them, "There's a right way, a wrong way, and the Benchmark way—and I only care about the Benchmark way." That philosophy still holds true today.

Our process is guided by a set of manuals that detail every aspect of how we operate. New leaders are trained rigorously in this approach. Over time, some individuals internalize it and excel. Others resist—and they don't last long. It's a process of constant refinement. Unlike companies that rigidly stick to their original product or process, we evolve and adapt. Those that don't, like some legacy restaurant chains, often fade away. Successful companies like Amazon are always looking for ways to innovate and improve, and that's the mindset we've cultivated at Benchmark.

When we hire a principal broker today, we promote from within. We don't bring in outsiders for these key roles because we want leaders who already understand our culture, our methods, and our way of thinking. We look for individuals who have been in the trenches with us, who have shown their dedication and alignment with our values. This internal growth ensures continuity and a deep understanding of our systems.

Once we select someone, we bring them into headquarters for training. Even if they've been an agent or a team leader with us, there's a lot they haven't seen. We pull back the curtain and show them the inner workings—the proprietary software and systems that power our business. These elements are closely guarded secrets, known only to a handful of people within the company, to protect our competitive advantage. (That said, it would take millions of dollars for a competitor to replicate what we've built, so the risk of someone leaving and being able to take this knowledge with them is minimal at this point.)

After the initial training and mentorship phase, we give our new principal brokers the autonomy they need to run their offices effectively. However, there's a clear expectation: Everything must align with the Benchmark way. We're all committed to continuous improvement, but we do it together. We don't allow independent pockets or rogue leaders to diverge from our core culture. This centralized approach is key to maintaining a unified company.

MAINTAINING A COHESIVE CULTURE

Many brokerages make the mistake of decentralizing their operations, effectively allowing each office to become its own independent entity. This creates a fragmented culture where the success of an office depends more on the individual broker than on the company's systems. In those scenarios, if a principal broker leaves, there's great risk they could take the entire office with them. At Benchmark, it's different. Our agents don't rely on any single broker's personal system—they rely on the *Benchmark* system. If a principal broker leaves, the agents stay because they're loyal to the company's proven processes, not to any one person.

This approach has been fundamental to our growth and resilience. It's about creating a scalable model that doesn't depend on individual personalities or preferences but on a shared commitment to excellence and a consistent way of doing business. By building a strong, unified culture, we've been able to expand without losing the essence of what makes Benchmark successful.

No matter what industry you're in, when your leadership is actively involved and there is a cohesive, centralized approach, you have control over the company's culture. But when you allow independent silos or "islands of difference" to form within the organization, things start to unravel. I've seen it happen firsthand.

A while back, I watched a perfect example of this play out. A prominent company merged with a couple of others, and the original founder—who had been the cultural heartbeat of the business—became largely absent. He spent most of his time at his multiple vacation homes in other states, far removed from the daily operations. Without his presence and active involvement, the company began to drift with cultural silos developing. Eventually, he came back to town—seemingly affronted by the way things had deteriorated in his absence—and started a new firm. He took over 400 of the original company's agents with him when he did so. It was a mess, and a dramatic turn of events for someone who should have been enjoying the legacy he had built instead of dealing with this upheaval in his seventies.

This is a sad example of what happens when a company is built around a single individual rather than a robust, shared system. It's why I emphasize that at Benchmark, we follow the "Benchmark way," not the "Phillip way." The goal is to create something bigger than any one person. If a leader fails to instill a clear structure, well-defined processes, and a strong culture before stepping back, the organization will inevitably drift. And don't forget that employees (or agents) left without structural guidance will fill the void themselves, creating their own interpretations of what should be happening. And that's when you lose control.

You need to build a system that stands on its own, a system that continues to function effectively even when you're not there. Your mindset must be about "we," not "me."

This concept was reinforced for me recently when a colleague of mine faced a similar challenge as head of the company she had founded. She initially made efforts to shift the focus from herself to the leadership of the organization as a whole, which was the right move. But then she changed her mind and tried to reclaim the spotlight, making everything about her again. The result? The company folded. It's a textbook case of what happens when a business is overly dependent on one person's identity rather than a collective vision.

I hear this a lot. People will learn about Benchmark's story and say, "Wow, what an incredible company you've built!" But I correct them every time: "It's not me; it's we." If it were just me, I'd have created nothing more than a job for myself, tethered entirely to my own energy and effort. But because it's "we," the company has taken on a life of its own. It's become a self-sustaining entity, carrying forward the vision and values we've instilled as a team and bringing a lot of good people along with it in a positive and powerful way.

To build a lasting business, you must create a structure and a culture that can thrive independently of any one person. It's about empowering your team, fostering shared ownership, and ensuring that the company's identity is rooted in a collective purpose, not a single personality. Do all this, and not only will you create a business that thrives now, you'll also set yourself up for a successful exit when that time inevitably comes.

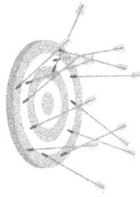

THIRTEEN

REACHING THE FINISH LINE

B Y 2018, WE HAD SOLIDIFIED OUR POSITION IN
greater Nashville, and we were just starting to extend
our reach into new areas like Clarksville. That's when the
calls started coming in from potential buyers interested
in Benchmark. Those calls initially took me by surprise, even
though I had positioned the company for visibility and recognition outside of our immediate geographic area. We'd spent

years building our reputation and participating in industry rankings like the RealTrends 500 as well as the *Inc. 5000*. In fact, Benchmark had been on that list for five years in a row. We had also been ranked as the 26th largest privately owned real estate brokerage in the country. But it wasn't about the accolades for me. It was about giving our agents a tool they could use to add perceived value in their client presentations. And it was about building credibility that would help them close deals.

For two years, I received phone calls from a wide variety of people, from large brokerage conglomerates to private equity firms, each wanting to do some sort of "combination deal." Their goals varied. Some wanted to sell us a franchise, others to purchase an equity stake or merge. Some sought an outright purchase of Benchmark Realty.

As a company with a large market share in the area, Benchmark was highly desirable. Fortunately, knowing that sooner or later some potential suitor would say the right words and hit on the right deal structure, we had been preparing for a sale. The company had no debt, no personal expenses buried in the financials (i.e. no private jets or company cars), and no personally owned real estate rented back to the company at inflated rates. We had intentionally maintained a very clean financial structure. And we were *very* profitable due to the operational processes we had installed and refined over the years.

Even though our financials were prepared, when the calls first started, I still had no true understanding of what it all meant and how to deal with it. The entreaties were numerous. There were so many different suitors flush with cash that I hesitated and then began to dread the phone ringing. Why dread? Because I finally realized just how clueless I really was. Eventually, dread turned into something closer to fear. This was unknown territory.

I'd been in the business world for thirty-five or so years at that time, so I knew how to run a company. I understand a profit & loss statement and balance sheet better than your average Joe, and having been through a lot of different stuff in the building of this company, I didn't think much could happen to cause me concern anymore. But I was wrong—this situation certainly did.

Realizing I had better get my head straight, I took a weekend alone to try to pinpoint exactly what was so unsettling about this process. At the time, I was in my late fifties. We had many factors pointing toward this being the time to do something, but the thought so troubled me that sleep was sometimes hard to come by (and as my family will tell you, falling asleep has rarely been a problem for me).

Then it hit me. My company and my "affairs" were not ready. Yes, we were far ahead of most potential sellers when it came to our financials, but we still needed to put things in the right box, put the right label on the right boxes, and then double down to ensure everything was as clean as possible.

I knew we could sell to anybody, but to get the best price and the best multiple, I needed to step up my game. Given my age, I only had one shot at this. Nailing the outcome meant educating myself better on the entire process and every miniscule variable that would make my company most attractive to potential suitors. So, I took myself back to "school," purchasing and consuming at least fifteen books on all aspects of M&A, with a focus on how to maximize the valuation of the acquisition target.

What I can tell you now is this: *Preparing a company to sell is tough!* Even with a company in as good a shape as mine, it became a second full-time job—and one that had to be performed in absolute secrecy. In our case, it required a realignment of the organizational chart, which meant getting the wrong people off the bus, the right people in the right seats on the bus, and then course-correcting for the proper destination. Honestly, all of those were things we should have been doing all along. And in many instances, we had been. But this was a whole new level of doing everything we should to get it absolutely right—and admittedly, we entrepreneurs rarely do every single thing we *should* do. Often, in fact, we do only what we *want* to do, or we react to circumstances as they arise.

This period of time was undoubtedly one of the most difficult of my life. In fact, the lack of knowledge and skills to prepare for a sale properly is why most company owners never maximize their return. It is so daunting a process that many simply give up and, consciously or otherwise, decide to just let their heirs deal with it. From this side of the journey, I can understand why.

CONTROLLING THE SALE PROCESS

As difficult as the exit process can be, the truth is every entrepreneur eventually separates from the ownership and control of the company they founded, even if the reason for that separation is death. Just as it is hugely irresponsible in our personal lives to not plan for what happens after our earthly departure, it is equally irresponsible for an entrepreneur to fail to plan for their inevitable company departure. Invariably, both will eventually happen, so there's no use denying it. As Mark Twain once said, *"Denial ain't just a river in Egypt."* Therefore, every entrepreneur has a responsibility to prepare, and this preparation should start years before the need arises.

I knew this, so my intention was to proactively control the process. A lot of families would be impacted if I got it wrong, most especially my own. Perhaps other leaders could live with themselves if mistakes messed up the lives and careers of others, but not me. It had to be done right, it had to take care of those who had placed their faith in me for all these years, and I had one shot at it. No pressure, right? Yeah...and now you see why I had come to dread those phone calls.

And then it happened. It was a sunny September day in 2019 when I received a call from Steve Murray of RealTrends (an industry icon and sometime-matchmaker) who said, "I've got a friend with a bag of cash who wants to talk to you."

That friend turned out to be Dan Duffy, the CEO of United Real Estate Holdings. After an initial conversation, Dan committed to a visit, and we planned for me to pick him up at TownePlace Suites in Cool Springs on a set date. If you are familiar with hotel chains, you know this is not exactly a Four Seasons. Clean and adequate, but not luxurious by any definition. That told me a lot about Dan's values. Now that I know Dan better, I am sure the hotel selection was an intentional statement.

I picked him up on a Thursday, in the middle of a downpour. We spent most of that day sharing our histories, our goals, and our aspirations. By the time I delivered him to the airport that afternoon, I felt we were really onto something. Despite that, I held to my practice of involving my wife in all major decisions.

Amanda's intuition is truly amazing, so when she gave her blessing to keep exploring this opportunity, I decided to take the next step. I made plans to visit United Real Estate's Dallas offices in December 2019 and spend some time with the leadership. While just an overnight trip, it was fruitful, and I returned with the feeling that our two companies were culturally compatible—and a rough draft of a Letter of Intent in hand.

The mention of "cultural compatibility" brings me to an important distinction that I think every entrepreneur should understand: the difference between the broad categories of *financial buyers* and *strategic buyers*. Financial buyers are focused on returns. They look at your business as a portfolio asset, something they can extract value from (potentially by cutting costs or even selling off parts of it). Strategic buyers, on the other hand, have a longer-term vision. They want to integrate your business into their own, leverage its strengths, and grow it further.

United Real Estate fell into the strategic buyer category. They wanted to expand using Benchmark as a cornerstone, but they respected our brand and our culture. They didn't want to rebrand us or make sweeping changes. In fact, they've kept the original brand identity of most every company they've acquired and refer to them collectively as a "family of companies." If you visit United's website, you'll see a showcase of all the different logos, each representing a business they've brought into the fold while allowing it to retain its unique identity.* That kind of

* https://www.unitedrealestate.com/family-of-companies

approach was exactly what I was looking for, and it's a big part of why I chose them.

DECIDING TO SELL YOUR BUSINESS

A frequent question I get from industry peers is, "Are you glad you sold your company?" I don't even have to think about my answer for a second. Of course I am—*the buyer gave me a bag of cash!* Kidding aside, this is usually followed by a more import-ant question: "How does the process of selling your brokerage work? Do you just throw a number out there and get a check?"

Not hardly, brother.

In selling a business, there are three general types of poten-tial buyers. I mentioned two of them already. First, there are *financial or cash-flow buyers* who are interested in the investment because of the cash the target business throws off. Then, there are *strategic buyers* who seek to leverage the forward momentum of the target to accelerate the growth of both companies. Finally, the buyer may be a *competitor* who is interested in consolidating or "rolling in" the acquired firm into their existing business in order to gain market share.

When it comes to strategic buyers, the contribution of the target firm to the acquiring firm's strategic plan has a strong impact on the valuation and can determine whether it is a good fit. The better the new firm dovetails into the existing firm strategically, the higher the valuation. In our case, United was a strategic buyer and we fit like a glove. They wanted us because they believed the synergy of the combined firms would propel both forward more rapidly, and it has.

Any merger & acquisition specialist will tell you there are as many ways to structure a sales process as there are people to do the deal. Each process is different, yet the commonality can best be described in a single word: *thorough*. Imagine your company being stripped bare and every nook, corner, and cranny examined with a magnifying glass—multiple ways, multiple times, with a constant refrain of, "Verify this for us."

I failed to grasp this concept when the other unsolicited offers began arriving, which undoubtedly led to the failure of some deals with potential suitors for Benchmark. Admittedly, I made the rookie mistake of taking certain questions personally, as if my own character were being questioned. Luckily, by the time United came along, I had learned a valuable lesson: **Never mistake intense questioning during the sales process as an insult to your credibility.** Pride can derail a lot of good opportunities.

For any entrepreneur who has invested years of blood, sweat, and tears into building a business, one of the hardest tasks is emotionally separating the business from your image of self-worth.

Yet, making this separation is absolutely necessary. In my case, the agonizing decision process—to sell or not, and to whom, when, and how—nearly drove me mad. You already know that without my wife's support and input, Benchmark would never have become what it is today. Without her counsel, this deal would have gone off the rails too. She helped me see that it really is just about business, and that knowledge enabled me to move forward when diligence got hard.

THE TRANSACTIONAL PROCESS OF A SALE

The *transactional* process of selling or merging a business all starts with a cultural meeting of the minds. Do you like the people you are dealing with, and can you trust them? Once that is clarified and found to be in alignment, there comes the signing of a very tight Non-Disclosure Agreement (NDA). Simultaneous with the execution of the NDA, the buyer will want to see three calendar years of profit & loss statements, the last three year's balance sheets, and a rolling twelve-month P&L. It is only after this verification of earnings that the prospective buyer can determine any sort of offering price.

An offer price is based on many elements, but generally there are three main attractors:

1. EBITDA – Earnings Before Interest Taxes Depreciation Amortization
2. The company performance trendline (going up or down, and why)
3. Does the company have sustainable recurring revenue that is relatively independent from the seller's own labor inputs—meaning, can the firm continue an upward trendline if the owner is no longer involved in production?

If these three elements are strong, the price offered to the seller is generally strong as well.

Typically, the initial offer price is a multiple of EBITDA. Not to sound vague, but in the real estate brokerage industry, that multiple can be anywhere from 2X to 5X, depending on the quality of the company, earnings consistency, the state of the industry, the company's market share, and the current market conditions. Profitable, well-managed companies with proven processes sell for higher multiples. Poorly managed companies with a mess in their back office sell for lower multiples, plain and simple.

Once the buyer is able to broadly verify the data they requested, they will issue a Letter of Intent (LOI). When the LOI is signed, the negotiations really begin. However, just like everything in real estate, everything in the LOI is negotiable. This document is non-binding and either party can throw their hands up and walk away at any time. So, by signing it, you haven't really agreed to anything except to walk through the investigative journey together, buyer and seller, under a general set of criteria.

While discoveries during the due diligence period can alter the terms of the final agreement, the buyer will generally want to stick to the original agreement as closely as possible. If you're going through a sales process, expect to give a little here and take a little there, with the LOI serving as the main roadmap for the transaction. That's why preparing your company ahead of time is so important. Nobody likes surprises, especially when *all* the chips are on the table.

A tip here before we go any further: You *must* have good legal counsel and a good CPA who both know the process and have experience with it. Your attorney cousin who runs the title company down the street may be a fine person, but they are probably *not* your best choice for the sales process. Likewise, the bookkeeper who has managed your books for many years may be loyal and a lovely person, but unless M&A is their area of specialty, they're not who you should use for this either.

Never scrimp on who you hire to protect your interests. I can attest to the fact that the experience of the attorney team I used (yes, it was a team) kept the process from derailing multiple times. Situations would arise where I was freaking out and felt like I'd had enough with the Great Inquisition. They would calm me down, saying things like, "In the deals we've seen, this is not a very onerous request from the buyer." Those conversations kept me from walking out the door several times. That and more is what *experience* brings to the table.

The purchase agreement comes next. Among other things, it details what the buyer must do, what the seller must do, what the seller must provide as part of the due diligence, conditions for closing, and representations and warrants for each party. These are basically statements of fact with a "warranty" that one party gives to the other certifying the information in the agreement as true, and if it later turns out to not be so, the party making the representation will make the other party whole. These are necessary because not everything can be verified on the front end.

A list of the detailed sections of a purchase agreement would be exhaustive and will vary from deal to deal. Suffice to say, every seemingly insignificant detail you know about your company, the buyer will also want to know. *Everything.* The final version of my purchase agreement ran more than seventy pages, with the disclosure schedules adding another hundred pages or so, all based on a due diligence process that took about six months. And you know what? Had I not purposely spent years preparing both the company and my own mindset for an exit, the time involved could easily have been double.

There are too many twists and turns in this process to be compressed into a few book pages. All I can say is, "No, you don't just throw a number out and get a check. Not even close."

My best advice to you here is simply this: Think long and hard about whether it's time to sell. If it is, educate yourself. Prepare your company. Take the calls and control the process. Do all that, and chances are high you will set a record for the multiple you get, just like we did.

VALUES AND CULTURE MUST MATCH

When you're selling your company, it is paramount to make sure you are marrying the right person! Yes, I used the word *marrying* because if you plan on hanging around after the sale, that's exactly what you are doing. You are committing to each other for the foreseeable future. The most important thing you can do in any deal is investigate the character of the firm and individuals with whom you're conducting the deal—not just for your sake, but for your people's. The more aligned you are in value and culture, the more likely the venture is to succeed following the sale.

Dan and I came to general terms in an LOI and began the due diligence efforts in early 2020. Both firms were heavily engaged in the discovery process when the world suddenly shut down in

March 2020. I will never forget the pained tone of Dan's voice the day we spoke and he said, "I'm sorry, but we need to press the pause button on this deal."

Aware of what was going on in the world, I was not surprised. Honestly, I felt kind of sorry that he was being put in this position. I had already invested $26,000 in legal fees, but I fully understood the need to put our pencils down. There was no choice. So we finished the call with a commitment to renew discussions as soon as a path forward could be found. In the meantime, we managed through the lockdowns and continued to grow our business, later accelerating out of it at an unbelievable pace due to pent-up demand.

Fast forward to late July 2020. I received a call from Dan asking if he could come down and take Amanda and I to dinner. We compared schedules and arranged a date. As a believer in speaking directly, as soon as we were seated, I asked him point blank, "Is this dinner about keeping Benchmark in play, or is it the big kiss goodbye?" It was a bold question, but whatever the response, I was braced for it. In any negotiation, it's important to always be ready to just walk away.

His equally bold response was that the visit was to keep us in play and pick up where we had left off in the discovery process as soon as a couple more issues cleared up in the economy. We enjoyed the rest of dinner and chatted amicably about the future.

Since he was staying at a nearby hotel, I volunteered to drive him back. As I was just pulling the car up to the front door of the hotel, and we were finishing our goodbyes, Dan reached down into his briefcase and pulled out an envelope. Handing it to me, he said, "Here is a check for your legal fees. $26,000. If it turns out we can't continue, at least you are covered."

I was stunned! It was unexpected evidence of strong character that clearly affirmed that these were people I could do business with. In response, I told him that if we did not close, I would cash it. If we did close, I would give it back to him.

We concluded the signing in December 2020 and shortly thereafter went to dinner again. This time, as soon as we sat down, I handed him back his check. I believe that when two people do exactly what they say they are going to do for each other, it's a good indicator of a cultural fit. If you and the people you are doing business with are not at this level of compatibility, walk away.

As we got deeper into the process, I began to realize that a critical part of any sale is knowing what comes next—for you, for your team, and for the business itself. Many entrepreneurs don't consider life after the sale until it's too late. They focus solely on the exit and miss the importance of planning for the transition. With each suitor, I had to ask, "What happens after the deal is done? What role do I get to play?" The suitors who couldn't answer that question with clarity didn't make it past the first conversation.

Dan Duffy at United Real Estate was the only one who gave me the right answer. When I asked him about my role post-sale, he simply replied, "What do you want to do?"

I couldn't have been happier to hear him say that! That open-ended response signaled a willingness to collaborate, and we worked together to shape a role for me that made sense for both of us. This approach was vastly different from others I'd spoken to, who seemed just a little too intent on stripping the company down, rebranding it, and moving on. Those suitors weren't inter-ested in the people who had built Benchmark alongside me—they were focused on the financial gain. But my team wasn't just a line item on a balance sheet. I'd raised them from the ground up, and I wasn't about to let them be treated as expendable assets. Dan understood and embraced this—a true value fit!

PROTECTING YOUR LEGACY

Looking back, the process of selling Benchmark was about more than just getting a good deal. It was about making sure the legacy of Benchmark and the continued success of our agents would endure. It was about building something sustainable that would carry on and thrive long after I stepped back. The decision to merge was carefully considered, informed by years of preparation, industry insight, and a clear understanding of what we had built. In the end, it was a validation of our approach: Focus deeply on the market you're in, dominate that space, and only then look to expand. That's how you build a business that lasts.

It's all about clarity. You have to know what you want before you even start the conversation. If you're only chasing the highest number, you may find yourself in a deal that doesn't align with your values or your vision for the future of your company. For me, it was never about getting the biggest payout; it was about finding the right partner who would honor what we'd built and take it to the next level.

And that's the real measure of success—not just selling the company, but ensuring its future is bright. It's about building something bigger than yourself, something that can stand on its own and continue to grow even when you're no longer at the helm. That's the kind of legacy every entrepreneur should aim for.

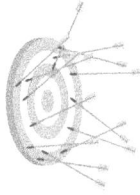

FOURTEEN

SPIRITUAL AND PRACTICAL PREPARATION

NTREPRENEURS, BY NATURE, ARE DRIVEN TO conquer, to plant flags, and to proclaim that no mountain is insurmountable. Yet at some point, we must confront our own mortality and the responsibility that comes with it. Many business owners wait too long to sell, often holding off until they near retirement and their energy levels are waning. By then, the business's valuation has likely dropped, sometimes significantly. This is why preparation is everything. You must begin the process early to ensure you have the stamina to see it through.

Of the fifteen books I read when I was preparing to sell, the three that stood out the most to me were *Finish Big* by Bo Burlingham, *Built to Sell* by John Warrillow, and *The Exit-Strategy Playbook* by Adam Coffey. Each of them offered real-world examples detailing what worked, what didn't, and why. If you're considering selling, start with these books. They'll help you get your mindset right so you understand the journey ahead.

Failing to do everything possible to prepare for a sale isn't just shortsighted, it's selfish. The people who have trusted, relied upon, and walked alongside you deserve better. What happens if you're not here tomorrow? What happens if you leave intentionally? What happens if something takes you away unexpectedly, maybe forever? These are not questions you can afford to ignore until the eleventh hour.

Once I realized that, I had an epiphany: **The process of transition, whether planned or sudden, requires deep emotional and spiritual preparation.**

The journey doesn't begin with spreadsheets or legal documents. It starts with introspection and prayer. You can't just wake up one day and decide to sell your company. Preparation starts long before the moment of separation. For me, that meant seeking guidance and clarity and leaning heavily on my faith. As you know, one of my long-time mantras was: *Compete with the man in the mirror.* Nobody could be harder on me than I was on myself. Perhaps that's a flaw, or maybe it's an asset. But I always take my struggles and uncertainties to the Lord, leaning on scripture and Bible readings to reset my perspective.

I've never worked with a coach or counselor in the traditional sense. Most of my lessons came the hard way, by smashing into walls and learning not to repeat mistakes. While that may not be the smoothest path, it worked for me. However, my preparation did include seeking advice from my pastor. Our regular lunches often served as informal coaching sessions, helping me think through the spiritual and practical aspects of leadership transition. Preparing for this kind of change requires humility and a willingness to detach from your ego. It also requires honesty about the state of your business.

Once the internal work is underway, the next step is to prepare your business. As I have emphatically stated, this isn't something you can start doing a few months before a sale. Now that I spend a lot of time evaluating acquisition targets from the other side of the table, I can see how common red flags are. Many businesses are often simply jobs the owner has created for themselves—and when your business is dependent on your constant involvement, that dependency will strip away significant value when you transition.

Other times, we may discover fourteen different ways the owner is getting paid, and all of them might be detrimental to the company's profitability. I've also seen owners pay themselves exorbitant rents for properties they personally own or hire relatives for roles that don't contribute meaningfully to the business. These deferred income streams may be fine for a company that will be closely held forever, but they wreak havoc on EBITDA and the valuation of your business.

That brings up an important point: If you own real estate tied to your business, you can't wait until the last minute to decide whether to sell it, move your company out, or rent it at market rates. These decisions take time and intention, and failing to address them can derail your efforts when it's time to sell. Remember, your buyer is going to review at least three years of financials, as well as a rolling 12 months backward from the date of the LOI.

Luckily, I avoided these kinds of situations in Benchmark from the start. I never owned the commercial real estate my company occupied. But for many, this entanglement can cost them dearly in a sale. You don't just lose the income stream from inflated rents, you lose a significant portion of your company's worth. However, by taking the time to separate your personal finances, streamline operations, and ensure your business can thrive without you, you honor the people who helped you build it—and you set it up for continued success.

In the end, preparation is not just about creating an appealing company for potential buyers. It's about leaving behind a legacy instead of a mess. And that, more than any flag planted or hill conquered, is what true leadership looks like.

PUTTING THE RIGHT TEAM IN PLACE

I touched on this earlier, but it bears repeating in a bit more detail here: Having the right deal team in place, particularly a skilled CPA and a knowledgeable attorney, can mean the difference between a smooth transaction and a financial nightmare. Many business owners make the mistake of relying on a friend, relative, or generalist for these roles. But selling a business is too complex for shortcuts. I was fortunate to have established partnerships with a CPA firm and legal team that specialized in the areas where I needed the most help. These weren't just one-person operations—they were teams with experts in real estate, corporate structure, and acquisitions, all coordinated by a lead professional. This team-oriented approach ensured that no matter the complexity of the issue, I had the right people guiding me.

The payoff for this preparation was immense. When it came time to sell, my transaction costs were astonishingly low—just $50,000 for both my attorney and CPA. But without the years of groundwork and the right advisors, those costs could have been three or even five times as much.

I cannot emphasize this enough: **Never cut corners when it comes to legal or financial counsel!** Early in my career, I didn't fully understand this. At Cantrell Graphics, years ago, we worked with a CPA who seemed great on the surface. Later, he was implicated in a land fraud scheme and ended up in jail. Looking back, there were signs and subtle cues that something wasn't quite right, but he was low-cost, so we let it ride. Fortunately for us, his troubles happened after we had sold the company and gone our separate ways, but that experience taught me the importance of trusting your intuition. As a business owner, you must develop a sense for when things don't add up. Ignoring that gut feeling can lead to costly mistakes. Over time, I realized that paying for top-tier advisors isn't an expense but an investment. A good CPA or attorney will save you money in the long run by preventing missteps, streamlining processes, and ensuring you're prepared for whatever challenges arise.

Even with the right team in place, selling a business is an enormous amount of work. It's not just the logistics but the emotional and mental strain of parting with something you've built.

However, the effort is worth it. Preparation and the right partnerships ensure that when the time comes to let go, you do so on *your* terms, with minimal complications.

A GRUELING AND INVASIVE PROCESS

I touched on it earlier, but I want to take a moment to talk a little more about diligence. Preparation has always been my strength, but nothing could have fully prepared me for the intense scrutiny involved in selling my business. Pardon the analogy, but it's akin to undergoing a proctology exam—*in public*. Every aspect of your operations, financials, and agreements will be repeatedly examined. Buyers circle back to topics you thought were settled, asking the same questions in different ways to ensure every detail aligns. And if there's any inconsistency, no matter how minor, it will be a problem.

This scrutiny is especially evident during the Verification of Earnings (VOE) process. Buyers want to see your sales figures over the past five years and validate them against invoices, contracts, and commission records. (A quick aside: You may remember that I initially wrote that buyers wanted to see three years' worth of financials. That review takes place during the LOI process and is part of setting the price they'll offer. The five years of sales figures they review during the VOE is part of due diligence). While the VOE process isn't quite as granular as inspecting every single invoice, it certainly feels that way. Every detail of your business is up for review, and there's no hiding.

The sheer level of scrutiny can feel invasive and even insulting. You may feel like your integrity is being questioned. It's easy to become defensive, but that mindset will only derail the process. You must approach it with patience (remember, patience is a virtue!) and a willingness to provide the answers buyers need, over and over if necessary. It isn't personal. It's simply how the process works.

As hard as that part of the process is, what caught me off guard the most wasn't just the depth of scrutiny but the confidentiality required. You naturally want to share the news with those who've been with you on the journey, but you can't. Until the papers were signed, the only people who knew about my sale were my attorney, my CPA, my wife, and me. Even my leadership team was kept in the dark until the deal was finalized.

The importance of this secrecy cannot be overstated. Sharing news prematurely, even with someone you trust, risks unintended leaks, which can quickly spiral out of control. Word can spread, damaging morale among your team and creating opportunities for competitors to exploit the situation. Keeping the sale confidential until it's complete is critical to maintaining control of the narrative and protecting your business.

STRUCTURING THE DEAL

One of the most important decisions we made during the sale of my company was opting for a Membership Interest Purchase Agreement (MIPA) rather than the more common asset purchase. An asset purchase allows the buyer to take only the assets while leaving the liabilities with the seller. It's a clean, straightforward approach for most transactions, but in our case, it would have been a logistical nightmare.

At the time of the sale, we had about 1,300 agents, each with an independent contractor agreement. An asset purchase would have meant renegotiating every one of those agreements, along with amending all active transaction contracts. Agents would have had to return to their clients to revise listings, purchase agreements, and ongoing deals—something I wasn't willing to ask them to do. Instead, I insisted on a membership interest purchase structure, in which the buyer acquires everything, including all assets, liabilities, contracts, and even the "warts" that come with the business. While this approach increased the scrutiny during due diligence, it allowed for a seamless operational transition. It was the only option that made sense for us, despite the additional complexities it introduced.

Negotiating this agreement structure started early in the process, even before the final letter of intent. The purchase document itself was enormous, reflecting months of back-and-forth discussions. The depth of detail was daunting, but it was necessary to ensure both parties were protected and aligned.

Once the deal was finalized, controlling the messaging became a priority. I used a prescheduled webinar to deliver the news directly to my affiliates, framing it as a positive, forward-thinking move. Simultaneously, a letter I had prepared was distributed to every member of our MLS, along with others in our industry. This coordinated approach ensured that the announcement was clear, consistent, and focused on the benefits for everyone involved.

Like many aspects of business, selling is an emotional and logistical marathon. It requires patience, transparency, and a commitment to doing things the right way, no matter how exhausting the process becomes. In the end, if you've done everything right, the effort will pay off, both in the successful transfer of ownership and in the assurance that the legacy you've built will continue to thrive.

AFTER THE SALE

Even after the sale, the transition from owner to employee isn't as simple as flipping a switch. Many entrepreneurs fear the loss of autonomy and dread becoming "just another cog in the machine." Because of my previous employment experiences, that was a very real concern for me, but it never materialized because of how I structured the deal.

The deal itself came down to a conversation—not a battle of wits or high-stakes negotiation but an honest, human discussion between me and Dan Duffy. Our ability to connect on shared values was of the utmost importance. Reputation, character, and integrity are what truly determine success in these moments. They're the things you do when no one is watching, and they set the tone for everything else.

I've always operated with a simple but unwavering philosophy: If I look someone in the eye, shake their hand, and give them my word, I will do everything in my power to honor that commitment. If I fail, there will be evidence of the blood, sweat, and tears I shed trying. I was determined to find a counterpart who shared that philosophy, and fortunately, I did. Without mutual trust, none of the details or creative structuring would have mattered.

The terms of the deal, including my two-year earn-out period, were unconventional, largely because of the condition and profitability of Benchmark. I received half the payment up front and the other half after two years, contingent on maintaining the same EBITDA as the day the deal closed. Unlike most earn-outs, which require aggressive growth targets, mine was based on stability. That's a rare arrangement, even with a great company, and it was possible only because of the trust and alignment I had with the buyer.

I also had clear priorities and a willingness to walk away if necessary. Remember: Never be afraid to walk away from the table. Enter every negotiation with the attitude that you have nothing to lose. And always be patient. Most deals come full circle when you approach them with integrity and persistence.

THE EARN-OUT PERIOD

The earn-out period is where many sellers falter. The earn-out period in a business sale is the time after the transaction during which a seller may receive additional compensation from the buyer based on the business hitting certain performance milestones. This allows the parties to secure part of the purchase price based on the company's post-sale performance.

However, in many cases, once a seller has a significant sum already in the bank, they tend to become detached. I suppose this is understandable, but it is also a serious mistake. You have to keep your foot on the pedal, not just for your financial benefit but out of a moral obligation to the team and business you've built. Selling doesn't absolve you of responsibility. If anything, it amplifies it.

During the earn-out period, I worked harder than ever. Before the sale, I had the freedom to be somewhat casual. If I needed extra cash, I could write myself a check. But once the deal was signed, that luxury disappeared. The P&L belonged to someone else, which meant every decision had to align with maintaining the business's value and ensuring the team's success.

Remember, selling a business is more than a transaction. It's a marathon that demands you maintain focus and energy even when it feels like you've already crossed the finish line. By staying fully engaged, you ensure not only your financial future but the ongoing success of the business and its people.

LIFE BEYOND THE FINISH LINE

The story of selling a business doesn't end with the final signature or the final wire transfer. That's just the beginning of the next chapter, a chapter few people talk about. Selling successfully might seem like a Hollywood ending, but what happens afterward is often far more complex. The first thing that was confirmed to me is that money really *isn't* the key to happiness. If you're expecting a big payout to bring you joy, you've already set yourself up for failure. Before the deal, I drove a 2020 Volkswagen Cross Sport, and I still drive it today. My wife upgraded to a 2023 Tiguan, but we didn't splurge on lavish rewards or make extravagant investments. Sure, I could have bought a Lamborghini for myself and every member of my family, but what would that prove?

Instead, I focused on practical decisions, starting with tax planning. For anyone navigating a sale, understanding the tax consequences is incredibly important. In my case, I had the option to pay taxes incrementally as the earn-out payments came in, or to pay them all up front at the current capital gains rate. It didn't take a genius to see that capital gains rates of 2020 were likely to rise in two years, so I bit the bullet and paid all the taxes up front. It was a tough check to write, but it turned out to be a wise decision. And it was made possible by a trusted CPA who guided me beyond the transaction itself.

Note: To be clear, this is not an offer of legal or accounting advice. I am simply relating what I chose to do. Your situation may be different, and you should seek the advice of a competent advisor.

The transition period also reinforced the importance of staying involved in the running of the business. Don't make the mistake that many sellers do—detaching once the deal is done, especially during an earn-out period. I worked harder during the earn-out period than I had in the previous two years. When you sell, you become accountable to someone else, and every decision has to prioritize the long-term health of the business. This commitment is what ensures stability for your team, continuity for your customers, and the full realization of the deal's value.

Ultimately, selling a business is a major pivot to a new chapter that demands just as much care, effort, and thought as the years you spent building that business. Success isn't about the payout. It's about how you carry yourself through the process and what you leave behind for the people and the company that got you there.

In terms of the money you make from the sale, my best advice is this: "It's not what you make—it's what you keep and how you invest it." Without a clear plan, even the largest payout can be squandered. For me, the first step was *discipline*. As a firm believer in tithing, I took 10 percent off the top and gave it to the church as we are instructed in the Bible.

After that, I turned to *financial planning*. I sought out an advisor who could handle the complexities of managing post-sale wealth. Selling a business isn't the same as managing personal finances. It's like graduating from selling small-town rental properties to brokering industrial complexes in New York City. You need someone with the right expertise for the level you're stepping into.

I made two real estate purchases, one for ministry and one for family pleasure, but beyond that, I avoided the trap of impulsive spending. It's too easy to let newfound wealth burn a hole in your pocket, which can lead to unnecessary purchases (a pool here, a luxury car there) until you find yourself without the financial cushion you thought you had. This is what frequently befalls lottery winners and, in some cases, professional athletes.

To protect my family's future, I set up a family trust. The assets are now structured in a way that minimizes tax burdens for our children when my wife and I are gone. The same strategic mindset that built a successful business must be applied here to ensure stability and legacy. My wife, Amanda, has been an anchor in this area. She genuinely doesn't care about money beyond meeting basic needs, and that perspective has kept us grounded. For us, money isn't a source of happiness. It's a tool we can use to make a difference in the world around us.

To me, money is nothing more than a measure of how well you're helping others achieve their goals. A scoreboard, so to speak. The more people you help, the more success you'll see reflected in your finances. But the money itself isn't the reward. It's the relationships you build and the legacy you leave behind that truly matters.

Luckily, Amanda feels the same way. However, not every couple shares the same view on money. That's why it's important for couples or partners to be aligned financially *before* the sale. Have that conversation early. Define your priorities—whether giving, investing, or saving—and stick to them.

One more tip here: In today's world of social media, it's tempting to announce your success to the world. But in reality, **your outcomes and results should be all the validation you need.** Social media is a great tool for building your business, but it shouldn't become a source of personal reward. If you use it for external validation, you'll find it's a bucket that can never be filled. Take a step back and ground yourself in something deeper.

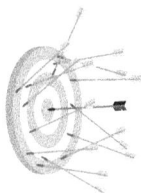

FIFTEEN

AFTER THE SALE

ELLING A BUSINESS IS A CULMINATION OF MUCH effort, planning, and timing. After all, "luck," as they say, "is what happens when preparation meets opportunity." For me, the sale of my business was exactly that: years of preparation meeting the right opportunity. When the time came, I was ready to take some chips off the table while still maintaining a relevant role in the company.

The best part of the sale for me wasn't the initial financial security for my family (although that was certainly nice), but instead the generational impact it created. As a business owner, most of your equity is tied up in the company, so the chance to diversify your assets is huge. For the first time ever, I could take a step back and know that my family was set for life. I had lunch with my two-year-old grandson recently, and the realization hit me: Because of the choices I made, his life will be vastly different from mine. That's a feeling I can't quite put into words. All the hard work I poured into the business will ripple out to create opportunities for future generations of my family.

Selling Benchmark was the capstone of my career, and it helped me create a legacy that will last. However, as rewarding as the sale was, it wasn't without its challenges. The hardest part has been the transition from being the sole decision-maker to being part of a larger organization. I'm still in a leadership role, but I'm no longer the independent "wild cowboy" who can make decisions on the fly. There's a layer of accountability and reporting now that didn't exist before.

For example, in the past, I might make salary decisions based on intuition or decide on year-end bonuses a couple of months out. Now, those decisions must be budgeted at the start of the year. While this is a small change in the grand scheme of things, it still requires more time and effort. Still, I've come to see this as a positive. It has made the business stronger and more disciplined.

That said, the transition hasn't always been seamless. The acquiring firm has private equity backing, which means they answer to investors. As a result, they sometimes need more data or justification than I would've previously provided. They've been respectful of my judgment, but there's definitely an added layer of formality that comes with working for someone else. And that has required me to translate all of the intuitive knowledge I had as the owner into a format that others can understand. Plus, I'm sure many within the parent organization view me as "uncouthly insubordinate" as they grapple with my driven personality and very direct communication style. (Sorry, everyone.)

When you've built a business from scratch, you have an innate sense of how things are going. Walking down the hall, you can feel the pulse of the company. Before the sale, I had a more fluid approach to running the business. I had heard of budgets, sure, but I didn't live by them. My philosophy was always revenue-driven: If you need more money, you roll up your sleeves and go get it. I've always struggled with the concept of a finite pie, because I've never been good at thinking in limitations. To me, targets are just starting points, always meant to be exceeded.

After the sale, I had to adapt to new expectations. And I have. My exit contract required me to stay for two years, but here I am four years later, still in a leadership role with the company. It's been an organic arrangement. The acquiring firm understands that no one knows this business like I do, because I'm the one who built it. And to their credit, they've respected that. But when the decision-makers are a thousand miles away, you have to transmit that knowledge in reports, spreadsheets, and projections. That can be difficult at times.

Despite the added effort, I see these changes as part of the growth process. In the end, selling a business is about balance. You must let go of some control while ensuring that the legacy you've built remains strong. It's not always easy, but when done right, it's deeply satisfying.

Of course, I'm well aware that I won't be in this role forever. That's why I've been preparing my successor...a process that has been going on for several years now. The first attempt, a COO hired externally, was a poor fit. But the second, an internal hire, has been much more successful. You already know that I believe internal hires have an edge when it comes to taking on leadership positions, and that's doubly true when it comes to appointing a successor. They understand the company's culture, processes, and rhythms. Your role is to teach them the nuances, the "steady hand on the tiller" that only experience can provide. And preparing them should begin well in advance of the sale, ideally two years before you step back. You're not simply handing off tasks. You are ensuring continuity for the business, your team, and the acquiring firm.

WHAT COMES NEXT?

With the company running smoothly and my family's financial future secure, I've started thinking about what comes next. I don't need another metaphorical whale to chase or an island to escape to. What I do have is a desire to share the knowledge I've accumulated, through both triumphs and painful lessons, with others. For now, that means writing this book, but it could also mean speaking, mentoring, or consulting. I've already started receiving invitations to speak at industry events, which is kind of cool. These opportunities feel natural because I believe in maintaining a strong network within the industry.

In the meantime, I have a house near the beach in Florida where I plan to spend part of my time, especially when it's 23 degrees here in Tennessee. But more than anything, I'm focused on staying relevant and ready to help others navigate the challenges I've faced. After all, selling a business doesn't mean stepping away from purpose. On the contrary, I now get to use the freedom I've earned to create a new kind of impact—to share what I've learned so others can achieve their own success. I don't know exactly what that looks like, but I remain open to whatever opportunities the Lord puts in my path.

The specifics of what comes next matter less than being prepared for change. Whether you stay in the same lane or chart a new course post-sale, make sure you have clarity on your priorities and flexibility in execution. You may want to jump straight into another venture, or you might focus on transitioning your role within the business or mentoring the next generation of leaders. Whatever you do, though, if you're staying on, resist the temptation to coast! A business is either growing or dying. There is no status quo. If you allow the company to stagnate, you're not only harming the people who supported you but also betraying the trust of the acquiring firm. You can't hand them an empty bag and walk away. To do so isn't just bad business, it's immoral. Far too often, I've seen business owners sell because they've lost the desire or capacity to keep pushing forward. They're burnt out and just want to escape. When that happens, buyers wind up purchasing a shell—a collection of used office furniture with no momentum behind it—and everyone loses.

So, even as you prepare for new opportunities, stay committed to the people and systems that built the business. Keep the business thriving. Most of all, pave the way for the future.

RESPONSIBILITY, LEGACY, AND GIVING BACK

No matter what stage of business you're in, as a leader, I believe our roles aren't just about decision-making—they're also about purpose. For me, giving back is a cornerstone of that purpose.

The Bible is clear: we're called to care for widows, orphans, and those in need (James 1:27). This isn't about seeking recognition or accolades but about fulfilling a deeper mission.

Matthew 6:1-2 reminds us not to perform acts of righteousness for the sake of applause. So, when I contribute to missions, tithing, or community projects, I don't trumpet my efforts. My reward isn't public acknowledgment, but the quiet satisfaction of knowing I've made a difference. And interestingly, I've found that the more I give selflessly, the more success flows my way. It's a cycle of reciprocity that's as humbling as it is profound.

When leaders lose sight of this responsibility, arrogance often follows, and with it, setbacks. Believe me—I've been knocked to my knees enough times to learn this lesson! When you thump your chest and take sole credit for your success, the fall is inevitable. True leadership requires humility and an understanding that your role is to serve others, including your team, your community, and those who rely on your organization.

If you want to experience *real* success, both in business and in life, then you must align yourself with principles greater than yourself. Regardless of your beliefs or faith tradition, you must see how your actions are part of a larger framework and understand that your success isn't solely your own. Your success is tied to how you contribute to the world around you. Indeed, this concept transcends religion. You don't need to share my spiritual convictions to grasp the idea that the universe operates on established principles. Call them whatever you wish: laws of nature, physics, or human connection. When you align with these principles, success follows. When you resist them, the struggle becomes inevitable. Think of it in terms of physics. You can't defy gravity, nor can you walk on the ceiling. If you attempt to operate outside the natural laws of the universe, you'll face resistance at every turn. For entrepreneurs, this means recognizing the value of humility, service, and connection with the systems, people, and environment around you. I have a strong faith that all of this was structured by God and given to us in His Word and his son Jesus Christ. You may not believe the same. Whatever you believe, though, you too can work to improve the lives of those around you and those that come after you.

One of the greatest obstacles to alignment is ego. Ego tempts us to believe that we're self-made, that our success is ours alone, and that we can bend the rules to suit our desires. It's a seductive but dangerous mindset. Trust me, I know: I've fallen into this trap myself in the past. When ego takes the wheel, it clouds your judgment and disconnects you from others. You start making decisions driven by self-interest rather than the greater good, and without fail, those decisions eventually backfire in some way.

The truth is, no matter how much we want to believe otherwise, we're all part of a larger system. Embracing that reality, whether through faith, reflection, or simply a recognition of interconnection, gives us clarity. And that, in turn, allows us to focus on the things that truly matter. Success, then, isn't about defying the laws of the universe. It's about working in harmony with them, aligning your purpose with the world's natural rhythms. The more you let go of ego and embrace this connection, the smoother the path becomes.

The path to success isn't glamorous. It's built on sharpening your saw day after day by polishing your skills and preparing for the challenges ahead. For those willing to put in the work, the reward isn't just success—it's transformation. And that's the real lesson. Greatness isn't handed to you. It's forged through effort, reflection, and the unrelenting pursuit of growth.

A FINAL WORD ON SUCCESS

Let me leave you with two final thoughts. First, remember this: The only place where we are all truly equal is in the twenty-four hours we're given each day. We each start with the same block of time, but what we choose to do with it is entirely up to us. The difference between mediocrity and greatness isn't talent or luck—it's how you spend those hours, day after day. The good Lord may give you the raw materials, but it's up to you to sand them down, polish them, and keep working on them until they shine like a gem. Persistence, hard work, and the willingness to refine your craft are what turn an ordinary idea into something extraordinary.

The second principle is just as vital: **Never be afraid to speak the truth, no matter how difficult it may be.** Your conscience is your compass, and when it tells you that something needs to be said, you owe it to yourself and others to speak up. But when you do, make sure it's the truth—and once you've spoken it, stand by it. Don't backtrack, don't waver. In business and in life, there's power in being honest and resolute. People can tell when you're speaking from a place of conviction, and it builds trust and respect. It's the foundation of authentic leadership.

These are simple lessons, but they've been the bedrock of my approach to building companies, making deals, and leading people. And if you keep them close, they might just become the cornerstones of your success as well.

THE MOST IMPORTANT THING

Now, there's one last thing I want to say—and it may be the single most important thing I write in this entire book: **Success is not found in pursuing our own ambitions alone; it emerges when we align ourselves with a purpose that serves others, creating value and impact that goes beyond ourselves.**

This is a guiding principle I've held onto through my journey, rooted deeply in a Bible passage that has spoken over me for many years:

Psalm 112 (NIV)

¹ Praise the Lord.

Blessed are those who fear the Lord,
who find great delight in his commands.

² Their children will be mighty in the land;
the generation of the upright will be blessed.
³ Wealth and riches are in their houses,
and their righteousness endures forever.
⁴ Even in darkness light dawns for the upright,
for those who are gracious and compassionate and
righteous.
⁵ Good will come to those who are generous and lend freely,
who conduct their affairs with justice.

⁶ Surely the righteous will never be shaken;
they will be remembered forever.
⁷ They will have no fear of bad news;
their hearts are steadfast, trusting in the Lord.
⁸ Their hearts are secure, they will have no fear;
in the end they will look in triumph on their foes.

⁹ They have freely scattered their gifts to the poor,
  their righteousness endures forever;
  their horn will be lifted high in honor.

¹⁰ The wicked will see and be vexed,
  they will gnash their teeth and waste away;
  the longings of the wicked will come to nothing.

Reflecting on this Psalm, I recognize that none of my accomplishments are solely "mine." I'm not sitting here thinking, "Look how smart I am," because that's not the source of my success. When I approach my work with the right intentions—focused on service rather than self-interest—everything seems to click into place. It's almost as if the pieces naturally align. But whenever I've pursued something purely for "Phillip's reasons," it's fallen flat, every single time.

The moment you start chasing money as your primary goal, you've already lost. Yet, success automatically follows when you place service, integrity, and purpose at the heart of everything you do. When your focus is helping others achieve their goals, whether those people are your customers, employees, or even your community, you're stepping into alignment with a greater purpose. And in doing so, you align with the natural flow of the universe—with the systems that, I believe, God put in place for us to succeed.

I've experienced both incredible highs and humbling lows in business. Out of ten businesses I've started, I've succeeded in four and failed in four (and "tied" in two). And each failure taught me the same lesson: When I wasn't driven by the right purpose—when I was focused on my own interests alone—things unraveled.

At the end of the day, success in business isn't just about strategy, skill, or timing. It's about heart. It's about serving others, helping them reach their potential, and making their lives better. If you come away with anything from this book, let it be this guiding truth: **Serve first, and the rest will follow. In business and in life, that's the principle that will bring you real success, and one that has the power to transform not only your career but also the lives of those you impact along the way.**

ACKNOWLEDGMENTS

I have contemplated writing this book for several years. So many conversations with friends who have heard my story have ended with, "You should write a book." Finally taking that to heart, I began this project in 2018, but multiple factors derailed my efforts. Many believe writing a book is easy. I can emphatically state that it is not. Writing a book requires hundreds of hours of labor, for me and for the team I relied on to see it come to fruition. Completing it is a great feeling of accomplishment.

A key player in the process of bringing this to life has been Kristin Clark, founder & CEO of Elite Content Creation, LLC/Cheval Press. Over many sessions we hammered this out together, and it has been her expertise that pulled it all into a format that would be understandable outside my head. To her, I cannot offer enough gratitude.

As I write this, we are at the final draft stage, so there is still so much more to go with the editing and production portions of the project. Those details will be handled expertly by Kacy Wren and others at Cheval Press. If you are reading or listening to this in an understandable format, they are responsible for that. In advance, I say, *Well done!*

As you most likely have figured out by now, I owe a lot to my parents—both of them. Even though Dave and Bettye have both been gone from this earth for many years, their legacy still lives in my heart and in the words contained in this book. My hope is that because of this work, their legacy will be carried forward to future generations.

Appreciation must go to all of the individuals who encouraged (and sometimes badgered me) along the way. A special thanks to author Dr. Jason Cruise, my ministry partner and pastor; to Dan Duffy, CEO of United Real Estate Holdings for the mutually supporting guidance and encouragement; to Scott Rowland, President of Benchmark Realty LLC; to the entire staff family for continuing to carry the ball forward every single day; and finally, to all of the licensed affiliates of Benchmark. Your support and loyalty have been a great part of my journey. Perhaps you can all glean something here to help guide you throughout your career.

If you paid any attention at all to my words in this book, you know how grateful I am to my wife Amanda. However, of equal importance to me are my children: Kellye, Sydney, Gus, and Libby (*listed in age order so as to not show favorites*). I love you all. This book is intended to be part of my legacy to you. And with that said, let's not forget my grandson, the amazingly intelligent and handsome Samson. Born on my birthday two and a half years ago, that kid has no idea what's in store for him. My family is my motivation for everything I do in life.

Finally, I am grateful to serve a loving Father who sent His son Jesus to redeem a lost world. Through my faith in Jesus Christ as my savior, I have been able to take on the challenges of this journey with much hope, and pay it forward for future generations.

ABOUT THE AUTHOR

Phillip Cantrell is executive vice president of strategy for United Real Estate. With over 25,000 agents and annual revenue approaching $20 billion, United is ranked as the #1 fastest growing residential brokerage in the country by RealTrends.

In 2024, Cantrell oversaw the launch of United's Financial Wellness Program, which has already resulted in personal debt reduction of over $3 million for the firm's affiliated agents. He is also Founder and CEO of Benchmark Realty, LLC, a thriving real estate brokerage with offices in Tennessee, Kentucky, and Alabama. In 2025, Cantrell ranked #163 in the Real Estate Almanac 2025 Swanepoel Power 200, a listing of the 200 most influential people in the industry. An alumnus of the Haslam

College of Business at the University of Tennessee, he and his wife Amanda call Tennessee home.

You can connect with him at *phillipcantrell.com.*

www.ingramcontent.com/pod-product-compliance
Lightning Source LLC
Chambersburg PA
CBHW071553210326
41597CB00019B/3223